ANTOINE BOUTERIN'S DESSERTS FROM LE PÉRIGORD

ANTOINE BOUTERIN'S DESSERTS FROM LE PÉRIGORD

Antoine Bouterin

with

Ruth Gardner

G. P. Putnam's Sons
New York

G. P. Putnam's Sons
Publishers Since 1838
200 Madison Avenue
New York, NY 10016

Copyright © 1989 by Antoine Bouterin and Ruth Gardner
All rights reserved. This book, or parts thereof,
may not be reproduced in any form without permission.
Published simultaneously in Canada

Food photos in insert by Ruth Gardner © 1989
All photographs are the property of Ruth Gardner © 1989.

Library of Congress Cataloging-in-Publication Data

Bouterin, Antoine.
Antoine Bouterin's Desserts from Le Périgord / by Antoine Bouterin
with Ruth Gardner.
p. cm.
Includes index.
ISBN 0-399-13468-9
1. Desserts. 2. Cookery, French. 3. Périgord (Restaurant)
I. Gardner, Ruth, date. II. Title.
TX773.B66 1989   89-10187 CIP
641.8'6—dc20

Printed in the United States of America
1 2 3 4 5 6 7 8 9 10

*To my mother
and my Aunt Jeanne
with love*

CONTENTS

1. Introduction   9
2. Basics: A Baker's Vocabulary, Tips and Importance of Hygiene, Basic Baking Utensils   11
3. Cakes and Entremets (Sweets)   29
4. Grandma's Country Cakes   57
5. Tarts   65
6. Desserts Made with Fresh Fruits and Vegetables   77
7. Crêpes and Soufflés   89
8. Breakfast and Coffee Break   99
9. Cookies   105
10. Conserves and Drinks   113
11. Desserts for Children   119

Index   123

CHAPTER 1

INTRODUCTION

When I was five years old, I baked my first chocolate cake for my sister Marguerite's birthday. While certainly not the best experience of my life, it was definitely an unforgettable one. Surely something very Proustian about memories and the scents and tastes of baking is what inspired me to write this pastry book with the wonderful assistance of my friend Ruth Gardner.

In Provence, the region of my childhood, there are not many desserts, but the cuisine is rich with a variety of scents and sublime flavors: the almond tart, the nougat, and the 13 desserts served for Christmas remain the most popular. The knowledge gained from my training in Provence has, throughout my professional career, enriched my culinary inspiration, as well as my pastry making.

Throughout this book I aim for simplicity: desserts that remind one of grandmother's cooking with natural, easy recipes to be used for special occasions, as well as with everyday meals.

A dessert must remind you of your childhood. Breathing the smell of caramel or hot rice pudding does that for me, just as the sublime taste of a banana pudding or a peach cobbler does it for Ruth Gardner. Her special recipes are treats from Arkansas, where she was born; they will surely become two of your favorite desserts.

MY PHILOSOPHY

In general, a dessert is the result of the pastry making. I believe that the recipe should be relatively simple, and that when you make it in your home, you should get as much pleasure from the process as you do from savoring the dessert at the end of a meal. And never forget that part of the pleasure is in changing ideas or inventing new ones according to your inspiration.

Mix everything and have a ball doing it!

PRESENTATION

The final look is an important part of the enjoyment, so always use a pretty serving dish, or decorate the plate attractively with flowers and fruits.

CHAPTER 2

BASICS: A BAKER'S VOCABULARY, TIPS AND IMPORTANCE OF HYGIENE, BASIC BAKING UTENSILS

A BAKER'S VOCABULARY

BAIN-MARIE OR HOT-WATER BATH: A container of boiling water in which another pot is set, as in a double boiler, on top of the stove, or a pan of hot water in the oven, used to cook food very slowly or to keep food hot.

BUTTER AND SUGARCOAT: To coat the bottom and sides of your baking dish, mold, or cake pan with butter, then to cover it entirely with a fine layer of sugar before placing the items into it to be baked. This method replaces the flour that is sometimes used in baking to prevent pastries from sticking to the baking dish.

BLANCH: To place an ingredient into boiling water for a few seconds in order to tenderize or soften it.

UNMOLD MOLD: To remove items from their molds and to place them on a grill to allow them to cool.

EGG WASH OR GLAZE (DORURE): The yolk of an egg beaten with 2 to 3 tablespoons of cold water and painted over food or pastry in light layers to create a golden color when cooked.

SKIM: To remove the scum that forms on the surface of milk or syrup during boiling.

GLACÉ: To sprinkle sugar on the pastries, then to place them beneath a hot broiler to obtain a layer of caramel that resembles a glaze.

PRICK THE BOTTOM OF A PASTRY SHELL WITH A FORK: This allows the pastry shell to cook without swelling.

TEMPERATURES: 250–300 degrees, very low; 300–350 degrees, low; 350–400 degrees, medium; 400–500 degrees, hot.

ZEST: The shaving of a lemon, lime, or orange peel produced by grating the peel, or thin strips of peel cut off the citrus fruit with a vegetable peeler.

NOTE ON TIMING: For boiling or simmering, cooking times always start after the ingredients have come to a boil. For accuracy, use an alarm timer that rings when the correct amount of time has passed.

TIPS AND IMPORTANCE OF HYGIENE

When cooking pastry, not only is it necessary to be well organized, but you must also attach a great importance to hygiene.

ORGANIZATION: First, you must read completely the recipe you are going to prepare. Then, set aside all of the utensils you will need, i.e., mixing bowls, molds, whisks, saucepans.

Next, you must weigh/measure all of the ingredients and set them aside in separate bowls so that everything is ready as needed.

The table or surface on which you work must be clean and should have only the items/ingredients needed for your recipe on it. Your cookbook should be open and protected by a plastic Plexiglas book stand, and placed in front of you in a manner that's easy to read. If you are baking and will need the oven, you should note the temperature required for the recipe and set it before you start to prepare the recipe. It should have reached the perfect temperature by the time you finish the recipe. Don't forget to use a minute timer with an alarm to ensure correct cooking time.

In general, it is preferable to unmold cakes when they are almost at room temperature. In any case, never place a hot cake or pastry in the refrigerator; wait until it is cool.

In pastry cooking, you should use ingredients in the exact proportions called for, and in the order in which they are listed. Changing any of those things can result in a different taste, a different texture, and can give you entirely unexpected results.

HYGIENE: For all cooking, your hands and nails must be absolutely clean, especially when working with pastry dough. You need a clean apron and a clean drying cloth. Make sure that all of the utensils are clean and dry, and do not carry any odors from previous cooking. For example, if you heat milk in a saucepan that was recently used to cook fish or garlic, you can bet that your dessert will have a garlicky or fishy taste if the saucepan has not been properly cleaned. The same goes for your hands and nails. If after careful washing, odors still persist, sprinkle a few drops of lemon juice, vanilla extract, or Grand Marnier in the utensil or on your hands, and wipe them with a paper towel or a cloth.

Carefully clean and dry your molds and other utensils after each use. It is even highly recommended to wrap them in wax paper between uses.

Use only fresh ingredients, and vanilla extract or vanilla beans should be used instead of artificial vanilla flavoring. Cream sauces and most recipes based on milk, butter, heavy cream, and fresh fruits should be used as quickly as possible.

If you freeze any of your pastries, do not refreeze them after they have been thawed for use the first time.

Wash your work space after each use, and be careful to use plain water; detergents should never be used.

BASIC BAKING UTENSILS

A plastic Plexiglas BOOK STAND. Allows you to cook with your book standing upright on your work space without its getting dirty; this makes following your recipe easier.

Two TART PANS with removable bottoms. Uses: For fruit tarts, pies, and pie shells. Sizes: 8"–11".

Round CAKE PAN, one-piece or with removable bottom. Uses: Basic cakes and sweets. Sizes: 8" or 9" diameters, with 1" to 1½" high sides.

Rectangular OVEN-PROOF GLASS BAKING DISH. Uses: Baked fruit, custards, puddings. Sizes: 1 pint to 4 quarts.

Two SPRINGFORM PANS. Uses: Cheesecakes, hard-to-unmold cakes, and tortes. Sizes: 9"–9½" diameter, 2½"–3" high sides.

A FANCY CAKE PAN, for different shapes, and more elaborate designs of cakes. Bundt and Kugelhopf pans are good choices. Uses: Pound cakes, yeast cakes, and fruit-filled cakes. Sizes: 9 cups to 3 quarts.

A wooden ROLLING PIN. Uses: Flattening pastry dough, and biscuit dough. Size: The heavier, the better.

A SAUTÉ PAN. Uses: For browning foods, stir-frying, poaching, and cooking sweets and sauces. Size: 10″–14″, preferably of a heavy aluminum material.

A SAUCEPAN. Uses: For blanching fruits, vegetables, cooking sauces and sweets. Size: medium, preferably heavy aluminum.

A SMALL, HEAVY CASSEROLE. Use: Cooking caramel sauce.

A TEFLON-COATED COOKIE SHEET. Uses: baking cookies, biscuits, and multiple small tarts in tart tins.

A STRAINER. Uses: Straining and purifying creams and sauces. The conical-shaped chinois in stainless steel is particularly useful.

FOOD PROCESSOR AND ELECTRIC BLENDER. Either of these appliances will do, as they can be used interchangeably. Either will save time and is quite handy for chopping, blending, and mixing everything from fruits and vegetables to cake and pastry batter.

ELECTRIC MIXER. Uses: Beating and whipping egg whites, cake mixtures, and cream sauces.

SOUFFLÉ MOLD. Use: Baking soufflés. Size can vary, but porcelain molds are preferable.

MIXING BOWLS. Uses: For whipping egg whites into meringue, mixing cake batters, and cream sauces. Preferably metal, not glass or plastic.

THE SMALL UTENSILS. An egg whisk, knives, a ladle, a skimmer, a pastry brush, tongs, wooden spoons, a grater, measuring cups and spoons, and a scale.

In pastry cooking, the shapes of your molds are important because often the cakes and sweets are named after the molds, or vice versa. To keep things simple, we have listed only items that are probably already familiar to you, easy to purchase, and practical.

DEMI-FEUILLETAGE PASTRY DOUGH

This fresh pastry dough reminds me of the wonderful, crispy tarts made by my Tante Gilette in St. Rémy, Provence. Later, at the restaurant Au Quai D'Orsay in Paris, I used this same pastry dough recipe to make my signature Tartes aux Prunes.

2 cups flour
½ cup unsalted butter, room temperature
2 teaspoons sugar
pinch of salt
4 tablespoons cold water

Sift the flour into a large mixing bowl. Add the butter, the sugar, and the salt. Using your hands, crumble the ingredients until the dough has the consistency of rough cornmeal.

Add 4 tablespoons of cold water, 1 tablespoon at a time. Mix and knead the dough until it is smooth and elastic, then pat it into a mound.

Sprinkle your work surface lightly with flour. Place the dough onto the flour and roll it out into a circle about ½" thick. Fold the edges of the dough over onto each other to form a rectangle. Let sit for 5 minutes.

Without unfolding the edges, roll out the dough and fold the edges over onto themselves to form a second rectangle. Let sit for 5 minutes. Repeat this step once again. Wait 5 minutes, then use according to your recipe. If precooking the pastry shell, follow baking instructions in the last 2 paragraphs of the pâte brisée recipe (page 16).

This delicate pastry is used for tarts, pies, millefeuilles, and any recipe calling for a light, crispy pie shell. The dough can be divided, frozen, and stored for later use.

PÂTE BRISÉE

This pastry dough can be divided and the unused portion frozen and thawed for use later. If you enjoy baking, it's a good idea to keep extra dough on hand for cooking last-minute pies, tarts, and other treats. Precooking the pastry shell prevents the dough from shrinking once you've added the filling. It also assures a fully baked, crisp crust for your pies and tarts. Be sure to prick the bottom of the shell with a fork and to weight it with beans or rice (this prevents swelling) before baking.

> 2 cups all-purpose flour
> ½ cup unsalted butter, room temperature, cut into ¼" cubes
> ⅛ teaspoon salt
> 2 teaspoons sugar (optional)
> 1 egg
> 6 tablespoons cold water

Sift the flour onto your work surface. Add the butter and the salt; add the sugar if you desire sweet pastry dough. Crumble the butter into the dry ingredients with your hands until the dough has the consistency of rough cornmeal.

Form the flour mixture into a circle with an opening in the center. In a small bowl, beat the egg and 6 tablespoons of cold water; pour the mixture into the center of the flour. Using your hands, quickly mix the ingredients and pat the dough into a mound. Gradually add flour 2 teaspoons at a time if the dough becomes too sticky. Wrap in wax paper and place in the freezer for 1 hour before using.

Preheat the oven to 400 degrees.

Butter a 9" removable-bottom tart pan; set aside. Remove the pastry dough from the freezer. Sprinkle your work surface generously with flour. Roll out a thin circle of dough, about ⅛" thick. Gently fit it over the tart pan; the extra dough will overlap the edges. Use your thumb and forefinger to press the dough around the inside of the tart pan. Pass the rolling pin over the top of the pan to cut off the excess dough. Use a fork, a knife, or your fingers to crimp the edges of the dough to assure that it fits tightly against the pan's rim. Prick the bottom of the pastry shell with a fork; set aside.

Lightly butter a sheet of foil. Fit it, buttered side down, into the pastry shell. Weight the foil with dried beans or rice; bake for 10 minutes. Remove the weights and foil, return the pastry shell to the oven, and bake 10 more minutes. Remove from the oven and set aside while preparing the pie filling.

MAKES TWO 9" TART SHELLS.

WHIPPED CREAM

Whipped cream, either regular or made with sour cream, is simple to make and can be used to spruce up all types of food. The regular cream is best suited for fruits, berries, chocolate cakes, ice cream, and tarts, while the sour cream mixture makes a wonderful topping for Tarte Tatin (page 69), warm cakes, and fruit compotes.

REGULAR:
2 cups heavy cream
4 tablespoons sugar
¼ teaspoon vanilla extract

SOUR CREAM:
1 cup heavy cream
4 tablespoons sour cream
3 tablespoons sugar

Pour the heavy cream into a cold mixing bowl. Beat at a high speed until soft peaks form. Add the remaining ingredients and blend for 1 minute more. Store in the refrigerator until ready to use.

SERVES 6.

CRÈME ANGLAISE

Crème anglaise is another easy-to-make, versatile sauce that can be used to "dress up" popular desserts such as cakes, soufflés, ice cream, fruit purées, and the well-known Floating Islands. The sauce is delicious served plain, or it can be gently flavored with liqueur.

1 tablespoon cold water
4 cups, plus 2 tablespoons, milk
1 vanilla bean, split in half
8 egg yolks
½ cup sugar

Place 1 tablespoon of cold water into a medium size saucepan. (This prevents the mixture from sticking later while it cooks.) Add 4 cups of the milk, set the 2 tablespoons aside, and the vanilla bean. Place a small saucer in the bottom of the saucepan (a trick used to keep the sauce from boiling over). Bring the milk to a boil over a medium flame; then turn heat down and simmer while preparing the rest of the ingredients.

Meanwhile, beat the egg yolks and sugar with an electric mixer until the yolks become pale yellow. Remove the vanilla bean from the hot milk. With the mixer on low speed, start to beat the egg yolks again. Add the boiled milk, little by little, to the egg yolk mixture.

Pour the mixture into a clean saucepan. Return it to a medium flame. Stir back and forth continuously with a wooden spoon while the sauce thickens; do not allow it to boil. Test readiness by dipping the wooden spoon into the sauce and running your finger across the back of the spoon. If the sauce runs back into the finger trace, it needs more cooking. If the finger trace stays clean, the sauce has cooked enough.

Pour the sauce through a fine sieve into a bowl. Stir in the remaining 2 tablespoons of cold milk and set aside, stirring from time to time until cooled. Refrigerate until ready to use.

If overcooked, this sauce becomes grainy. To rescue it, pour the mixture into a bottle or jar. Add 2 tablespoons of milk or heavy cream and shake for 20 seconds. Pour into a large bowl, stirring constantly to cool it so it doesn't continue to cook.

MAKES 3 CUPS.

CRÈME PÂTISSIÈRE

1 tablespoon cold water
4 cups milk
1 vanilla bean, split
8 egg yolks
½ cup sugar
1 cup flour

Place 1 tablespoon of cold water into a medium size saucepan. (This prevents the mixture from sticking later while it cooks.) Add the milk and the vanilla bean. Place a small saucer into the bottom of the saucepan (this prevents the sauce from boiling over). Bring the milk to a boil over a medium flame; then turn heat down and simmer while preparing the rest of the ingredients.

Meanwhile, beat the egg yolks and sugar with an electric mixer until the yolks become pale yellow. Sift the flour into the mixture and stir with a whisk until it becomes creamy and very pale yellow. Remove the vanilla bean from the hot milk. With the mixer on low speed, add the boiled milk, little by little, to the egg yolk mixture. Pour the mixture into a clean saucepan. Over a medium flame, stir back and forth continuously with a wooden spoon until the sauce thickens to a creamy, pudding-like consistency. With a spoon, force the sauce through a fine sieve into a bowl. Stir it so it settles evenly in the bowl.

Rub a stick of unsalted, room-temperature butter lightly across the top of the crème to prevent it from hardening and forming a skin. Set aside to cool. Repeat this step two more times, stirring the mixture, then passing the butter over the top. Use a spatula to remove all of the crème sauce from the sides of the bowl.

To make a lighter crème, when it has cooled, stir in 3–4 tablespoons of whipped cream.

It can be served as a filling for a génoise, or as a topping or an accompaniment for any simple cake.

MAKES 3 CUPS.

VERY SIMPLE GÉNOISE CAKE

This is truly an easy-to-make sponge cake. It is the basis for many different filled cakes, and can be cut into layers, as well as covered with creams, fruit purées, and icings.

> *5 eggs*
> *½ cup sugar*
> *½ cup flour*
> *½ teaspoon baking powder*

Preheat the oven to 350 degrees.

Butter and sugarcoat a 9″ springform cake pan; set aside.

Place the eggs into a large mixing bowl. Add the sugar. Beat at a high speed with an electric mixer for about 5 minutes, or until the mixture has a mousse-like consistency. Set aside.

Sift the flour into another large mixing bowl; add the baking powder. Gently fold the egg mixture into the flour with a rubber spatula. Pour the mixture into the cake pan. Cook for 30–35 minutes, or until a toothpick stuck into the center of the génoise comes out clean.

SERVES 8.

CARAMEL SAUCE

1 cup sugar
⅓ cup water

Melt the sugar in ⅓ cup of water over high heat. The caramel will turn light brown after about 5–6 minutes. Remove from the heat to prevent it from burning. The sauce should remain soft and liquid. Use quickly before it hardens.

MAKES 1 CUP OF SAUCE.

STRAWBERRY OR RASPBERRY SAUCE

1 pint of fresh or frozen strawberries or raspberries
1 tablespoon fresh lemon juice
2 tablespoons sugar
4 tablespoons cold water

Wash the berries; drain them in a colander. In the bowl of a food processor, place the berries with the lemon juice, sugar, and 4 tablespoons of cold water. Process into a purée. Strain through a sieve into a bowl, and the sauce is ready to complement a cake, soufflés, fruits, ice creams, or compotes. Otherwise, refrigerate until ready to use.

MAKES ABOUT 1½ CUPS OF SAUCE.

APPLE SAUCE

*2 large Granny Smith apples, peeled, cored, and
    quartered
3 tablespoons sugar
1 teaspoon vanilla extract
¾ cups water*

Dice the quartered apples into small pieces and place into a medium size saucepan. Add the sugar, vanilla extract, and water. Cook about 20 minutes over a medium flame. Mash with a fork and serve immediately (using a fork gives you a coarser texture, which is preferable to the sometimes overly smooth results obtained with a food processor). This sauce can also be stored in the refrigerator and used over several days.

MAKES ABOUT 1½ CUPS.

PLUM SAUCE
(ALSO GOOD WITH APRICOTS, NECTARINES)

8 fresh, ripe plums, pitted and sliced
2 tablespoons sugar
1 tablespoon fresh lemon juice
6 tablespoons cold water

Wash and dry the fruit. Place the fruit, the sugar, the lemon juice, and 6 tablespoons of cold water into the bowl of a food processor. Process about 2 minutes, or until mixture becomes a purée. Force through a sieve with a spoon. Refrigerate until ready to serve.

MAKES ABOUT 1½ CUPS OF SAUCE.

POACHED PEAR

6 cups hot water
1½ cups sugar
1 vanilla bean, split
2 lemons, 1 quartered, 1 halved
6 fresh pears, peeled, cored, and halved

Place 6 cups of hot water into a large saucepan. Add the sugar, the vanilla bean, and the lemon quarters. Bring to a boil over a high flame.

Place the pears into a bowl. Squeeze the juice of the half lemon over them to prevent the pears from turning brown. Set aside.

When the water begins to boil, add the pears. Set a heat-resistant plate on top of the pears to keep them submerged (otherwise, the pears will float to the top). Reduce the flame and boil slowly for 30 minutes. Eventually, the water will thicken into a syrup.

Remove the pears from the syrup and place into a large serving bowl. The syrup can be used as a caramel by heating it over a high flame until it reduces further and becomes thick and golden; or it can be covered and stored in the refrigerator and reused to poach other fruits. Serve the pears alone as a dessert, or as an accompaniment to a plain cake.

SERVES 12.

AN EASY PÂTE À BEIGNET

For me, the pâte à beignet remains one of the easiest basic pastry recipes. It's one that allows you to transform simple fruits into sublime desserts; and besides, who among us doesn't carry a childhood memory of the odor and the taste of a hot apple beignet covered in sugar?

>1 cup beer
>1½ cups flour
>⅛ teaspoon salt
>3 egg whites
>1 tablespoon sugar

Pour the beer into a large mixing bowl and sift in the flour. Add the salt.

In a cool bowl, whip the egg whites until soft peaks form. Add the sugar and continue to whip until the peaks become stiff.

Fold the whipped egg whites into the beer mixture. Blend well. This pâte à beignet should be used immediately and cannot be stored for later use.

MAKES 2 CUPS OF MIXTURE.

LADYFINGERS

5 egg yolks
8 egg whites
1 cup sugar
2 teaspoons vanilla extract
2 cups flour
1 tablespoon confectioners' sugar
zest of 1 lemon or orange (optional)

Preheat the oven to 350 degrees.

Place the egg yolks and the egg whites into large, separate mixing bowls. Add ⅓ cup of the sugar to the egg yolks and the remaining sugar to the egg whites.

In a cool bowl, beat the egg yolks and sugar with an electric mixer until they become pale yellow and fluffy. Add the vanilla extract. Beat the egg whites and sugar until they form still peaks. Gently fold the fluffy egg yolks into the egg whites. Sift in the flour, mixing with a rubber spatula.

Place the mixture into a pastry bag with a size 10 tube opening. Squeeze out rows of 4"-long ladyfingers onto a non-stick cookie sheet. Bake for 5 minutes. Remove and sprinkle with confectioners' sugar.

To make a basic ladyfinger belt, squeeze out rows of 2"-long, closely spaced ladyfingers the entire length of the cookie sheet; cookies will melt and spread so that the sides join together to form a "belt" when cooked. Bake and use as needed.

MAKES ABOUT 60 LADYFINGERS.

TULIP SHELLS

Tulip desserts on restaurant menus remain quite "in" despite the fact that they've been around for a long time. It's a pretty, yet practical way to serve sherbet and fresh fruit such as berries, and it's always a pleasant surprise to see the delicate form of the tulip. In short, it's versatile, easy to make, and all but guarantees you a successful dinner.

> 1 cup egg whites, about 6 egg whites
> 1 cup confectioners' sugar
> 1 cup melted, unsalted butter
> 1 teaspoon vanilla extract
> ¾ cup flour

Preheat the oven to 350 degrees.

Needed: Four small bowls, or ramekins, that fit into each other.

Combine the egg whites and the sugar, the butter, and the vanilla extract in the bowl of a processor; sift in the flour and process until combined. Pour the mixture into a bowl and refrigerate for 2 hours. This batter can also be prepared 1–2 days in advance.

Pour a tablespoon of the batter onto a non-stick cookie sheet. Using circular movements, spread the mixture with the spoon to create a small circle. Repeat these steps and make a second circle. Bake for 10 minutes.

With a flat metal spatula, lift the hot pastry circles from the cookie sheet. Turn two of the bowls upside down and place a pastry circle over the bottom of each inverted bowl. Cover each bowl with a second bowl, and press down gently to form the tulip shell. Let them cool and harden, then remove the shells from the bowls and place them on a flat surface. Continue baking in pairs until all batter is used. Serve filled with fresh fruits, ice cream, or sherbet.

SERVES 8–10.

CHAPTER 3
CAKES AND ENTREMETS (SWEETS)

COCONUT CAKE

5 eggs
1½ cups sugar
1 tablespoon rum
½ cup flour
2 cups grated coconut
1 tablespoon baking powder
4 tablespoons unsalted butter, room temperature

Preheat the oven to 350 degrees.
   Butter a 1½ quart baking dish and set it aside.
   Whisk the eggs and sugar together in a medium size mixing bowl. Add the rum, sift in the flour, and blend. Mix in the coconut, then the baking powder and the butter.
   Pour the mixture into the baking dish. Bake for 30–40 minutes. Allow to cool and serve alone or with ice cream.

SERVES 8.

PLAISIR DES ABEILLES

1 cup honey
8 eggs
2 cups flour
1¼ cups hazelnuts or filbert nuts
2 tablespoons unsalted butter, melted

Preheat the oven to 300 degrees.

In a mixing bowl, whisk together the honey and eggs. Sift in the flour and blend again.

Place the nuts into the bowl of a processor and process them into fine crumbs. Add the nut crumbs and the butter to the batter and blend.

Butter a 1½ quart baking dish and pour the batter into it. Bake for 35 minutes.

Serve warm with whipped cream (page 17) mixed with a tiny bit of honey, and of course, a cup of coffee.

SERVES 8.

LEMON BREAD

4 eggs (2 entire eggs, plus 2 yolks only; reserve the 2 egg whites)
¾ cup sugar, plus 1 tablespoon
1 cup flour
zest of 2 lemons
½ teaspoon baking powder

LEMON BUTTER
juice of 1 lemon, about 1 tablespoon
2 tablespoons soft butter
1 tablespoon sugar

Bread: Butter and sugarcoat a 9″ × 4″ × 3″ bread loaf pan; set aside.

Place the entire eggs, the egg yolks, and ¾ cup of the sugar in a mixing bowl. Hold the extra tablespoon of sugar aside. Beat until the egg mixture becomes pale yellow and creamy. Sift in the flour, the zest, and the baking powder; blend with a rubber spatula.

Whip the egg whites until soft peaks form. Add the remaining tablespoon of sugar and whip until the peaks become stiff.

Using a rubber spatula, gently fold the egg whites, little by little, into the batter. Pour the batter into the pan and bake for 20 minutes.

In the meantime, make the lemon butter. In a small bowl, add the lemon juice, the butter, and the sugar. Use a fork to blend the ingredients until the mixture becomes creamy.

Remove the bread from the oven, unmold, and serve hot with the lemon butter. This bread can also be wrapped in wax paper and will keep in the refrigerator for several days.

SERVES 8.

BRIOCHE TROMPE L'OEIL

1 teaspoon active dry yeast
1 cup, plus 1¾ tablespoons sugar
2½ tablespoons warm water
2 entire eggs
1 cup flour
5 tablespoons melted, unsalted butter
4 egg whites

Preheat the oven to 350.

Butter and sugarcoat a 1½ quart baking dish; set aside.

Combine the yeast, ½ teaspoon of the sugar, and 2½ tablespoons of warm water in a cup and set aside, covered, in a warm area for 10 minutes to allow it to rise.

Whisk the eggs and 1 cup of the sugar together in a large bowl. Sift in the flour and mix. Stir in the butter and set aside.

Beat the egg whites with an electric mixer until soft peaks form. Add the remaining sugar and beat until the peaks become stiff.

Add the yeast mixture to the flour mixture and blend. Fold in the egg whites.

Pour the mixture into the baking dish leaving 1″ at the top of the rim. Any leftover batter can be cooked in a small baking dish. Refrigerate for 20 minutes.

Bake for 30 minutes. Unmold immediately and serve with a little butter. For a fancier cake, bake it in a 3½″ × 6½″ Kugelhopf cake pan.

SERVES 8.

PISTACHIO PUDDINGS

⅓ cup pistachio nuts, shelled and coarsely ground
4 tablespoons sugar
4 tablespoons Kirsch liqueur
2 tablespoons unsalted butter, room temperature
4 tablespoons almond powder
1 cup warm water
20 ladyfingers cut in half horizontally (page 26)

Use a rubber spatula to mix the ground nuts and the sugar in a mixing bowl. Stir in 2 tablespoons of the liqueur, the butter, and the almond powder. If necessary, use your hands to mix the ingredients.

In a small bowl, mix together the remaining 2 tablespoons of Kirsch and 1 cup of warm water. Dip each of the halved ladyfingers into this mixture and line the sides and bottoms of 6 individual 3″ × 1½″ ramekins with them.

Fill each ramekin with the nut mixture. Refrigerate for 3 hours.

Unmold the "pâte à pistache," sprinkle with confectioners' sugar, and serve with a crème anglaise flavored with Kirsch (page 18).

SERVES 6.

WHITE WINE CAKE

12 slices white bread
½ cup dry white wine
3 entire eggs
3 egg yolks
½ cup, plus 2 tablespoons, sugar
3 egg whites

Preheat the oven to 350 degrees.

Butter and sugarcoat a 1½ quart baking dish; set aside.

Place the bread slices into the bowl of a food processor and process into fine crumbs. Pour the crumbs into a large mixing bowl. Add the wine, the 3 eggs, and the 3 egg yolks; reserve the 3 remaining egg whites. Use a wooden spoon to mix the ingredients. Stir in ½ cup of the sugar, reserving the other 2 tablespoons.

In a cool bowl, whip the egg whites until soft peaks form. Add the remaining 2 tablespoons of sugar and beat again until the peaks become stiff. Gently fold the whipped egg whites into the bread crumb mixture. Pour into the baking dish and place it in a bain-marie. Bake for 30 minutes.

Serve hot with apple sauce (page 22) or with coffee and some light whipped cream (page 17).

SERVES 8.

CHOCOLATE CHIP CAKE

¾ cup flour
1½ teaspoon baking powder
½ teaspoon cinnamon
1 teaspoon vanilla extract
3 tablespoons cognac
⅓ cup sugar
3 tablespoons heavy cream
3 tablespoons milk
3 eggs
¾ cup unsalted butter, melted
¾ cup small chocolate chips

Preheat the oven to 350 degrees.

Butter and sugarcoat a 3" × 9" loaf pan; set aside.

Combine the flour, baking powder, cinnamon, vanilla extract, cognac, sugar, cream, milk, eggs, and butter in the bowl of a food processor. Process until the mixture is smooth and creamy.

Pour the cake batter into the pan. Sprinkle the chocolate chips evenly over the top of it (use the smallest chips available, otherwise they will settle to the bottom of the pan and cause the cake to stick). Bake for 30 minutes.

Unmold and allow to cool before serving.

SERVES 6.

CRÈME BRÛLÉE

2 cups heavy cream
1 tablespoon vanilla extract
5 egg yolks
½ cup sugar
3 tablespoons brown sugar

Preheat the oven to 250 degrees.

Combine the heavy cream and the vanilla extract in a saucepan and heat over a medium flame. Do not allow it to boil.

Whisk the yolks and the sugar in a mixing bowl until the mixture becomes pale yellow.

When the milk is very hot, stir it gradually into the egg mixture. Pour the mixture into a 1½ quart baking dish. Place the baking dish in a hot bain-marie; bake for 50–60 minutes.

Remove the crème brûlée from the oven and allow it to cool.

Turn the oven to broil. Sift the brown sugar over the top of the crème, then broil it until the sugar melts and turns golden brown. Can be served warm or cold.

To vary the flavorings, add 1 teaspoon of coffee extract (found in supermarkets) or 2 teaspoons of chocolate syrup to the mixture just before stirring into the hot milk.

SERVES 6.

ORANGE CHOCOLATE CHIP CAKE

1 cup flour
1 teaspoon baking powder
½ teaspoon cinnamon
1 tablespoon vanilla extract
½ cup sugar
6 tablespoons melted, unsalted butter
3 eggs
2 tablespoons rum
3 tablespoons milk
3 tablespoons heavy cream
½ cup small chocolate chips
zest of 1 orange

Preheat the oven to 350 degrees.

Butter and sugarcoat a 1½ quart baking dish; set aside.

Sift the flour into a large mixing bowl. Use a whisk to beat in the baking powder, cinnamon, vanilla extract, sugar, butter, and eggs; set aside.

In a small bowl, mix together the rum, the milk, and the heavy cream. Add to the batter along with the chocolate chips and the orange zest and blend. Pour the batter into the baking dish and bake for 30 minutes. Unmold; set aside to cool before serving.

SERVES 8.

LIGHT CHEESECAKE

½ cup Nilla wafer crumbs (made by crushing 15 Nilla wafer cookies into fine crumbs)
4½ tablespoons sugar
1 cup cream cheese
1 cup cottage cheese
1 cup sour cream
4 eggs
zest of 2 lemons
1 teaspoon vanilla extract

WHIPPED CREAM TOPPING:
2 cups heavy cream
3 tablespoons sugar
3 tablespoons maple syrup

Preheat the oven to 400 degrees.

Butter a 9" springform cake pan. Coat with the cookie crumbs, then sprinkle the bottom of the pan with ½ tablespoon of the sugar.

Place the cream cheese, cottage cheese, sour cream, eggs, and the remaining sugar into the bowl of a processor. Process for 20 seconds. Add the lemon zest, vanilla extract, and process again for 20 seconds. Use a rubber spatula to scrape the sides of the processing bowl.

Pour the mixture into the cake pan. Bake for 15–20 minutes. Remove; set aside to cool to room temperature.

Whipped cream topping: Use an electric mixer to whip the heavy cream in a medium size mixing bowl until stiff peaks form. Add the sugar; beat thoroughly. Beat in the maple syrup. Refrigerate until ready for use.

Cake: Use a knife to separate the sides of the cooled cheesecake from the cake ring. Unmold the cake onto a serving platter. Use a knife or a spatula to cover the top and sides of the cake with the whipped cream.

SERVES 8.

VANILLA ICE CREAM
Without an Ice Cream Maker

2 cups milk
1 vanilla bean, split
4 egg yolks
½ cup sugar
4 tablespoons whipped cream (page 17)
1 egg white, whipped until fluffy

Bring the milk and the vanilla bean to boil in a medium size saucepan.

Meanwhile, whisk the egg yolks and sugar in a mixing bowl until the yolks become pale yellow. Remove the vanilla bean from the hot milk. Begin to whisk the egg yolks again. Add the boiled milk, little by little, to the egg yolk mixture. Blend well.

Pour the mixture into a clean saucepan. Over a medium flame, with a wooden spoon, stir back and forth continuously while the cream sauce thickens; do not allow it to boil. Test readiness by dipping the wooden spoon into the sauce and running your finger across the back of the spoon. If the cream sauce runs back into the finger trace, it needs more cooking. If the finger trace stays clean, it has cooked enough.

Pour the cream sauce through a fine sieve into a bowl. Set aside to cool, stirring occasionally. When cooled, fold in the whipped cream and the beaten egg white. Place it in the freezer, stirring occasionally until it begins to freeze. After about 4 hours, when completely frozen, serve the glacé using a large spoon.

Note: When overcooked, this sauce becomes grainy. To recover it, pour the mixture into a bottle or jar. Add 2 tablespoons of milk or heavy cream and shake for 20 seconds. Pour into a large bowl, stirring to cool it so it doesn't continue to cook.

SERVES 4–6.

COUNTRY PRUNE FLAN

12 ounces pitted prunes
5 eggs
1 cup sugar
¾ cup flour
½ teaspoon baking powder
¼ teaspoon vanilla extract
1½ cups milk
1 tablespoon dark rum (optional)

Preheat the oven to 400 degrees.

Butter and sugarcoat a 9" cake pan. Spread the prunes evenly over the bottom of the pan; set aside.

Use a whisk to beat the eggs and sugar together. Sift the flour into the mixture and beat. Mix in the baking powder, vanilla extract, milk, and rum. Pour the mixture over the prunes. Bake for 40 minutes, or until a toothpick stuck into the cake comes out clean.

Unmold the cake upside down onto a serving dish. Allow to cool before serving.

SERVES 6.

DIPLOMATE MINUTE

3 eggs
½ cup sugar
1 teaspoon vanilla extract
1½ cups milk
½ roulé cake (page 45)

Preheat the oven to 350 degrees.

Butter and sugarcoat a 9″ cake pan; set aside.

Whisk the eggs, the sugar, the vanilla extract, and the milk in a mixing bowl. Break the roulé cake into small pieces and stir gently into the mixture until the cake is saturated.

Pour into the cake pan. Place into a hot bain-marie and bake in the oven for 30 minutes.

Cool, then serve with crème anglaise (page 18).

SERVES 6.

CHESTNUT MOUSSELINE

CARAMEL (OPTIONAL):
¼ cup hot water
½ cup sugar

MOUSSELINE:
1 cup purée de marrons (chestnut paste)
8 tablespoons sugar
1 tablespoon rum
6 tablespoons hot milk
1 vanilla bean, split
4 tablespoons melted, unsalted butter
3 egg whites

Preheat the oven to 350.

Caramel: Heat the sugar and the hot water in a saucepan over a high flame until it caramelizes and turns golden brown. Pour the liquid into a 1½ quart baking dish. Hold the dish and swish it around to coat the bottom and sides with the caramel. Set the dish aside to allow the caramel to cool. If you prefer to skip this step, just butter and sugarcoat the dish to prevent the mousseline from sticking.

Mousseline: Stir the chestnut paste in a large mixing bowl to separate it. Stir in 6 tablespoons of the sugar and the rum and set aside. Heat the milk and the vanilla bean in a small saucepan over a low flame; do not allow it to boil. Add this mixture and the butter to the ingredients in the mixing bowl. Stir with a rubber spatula, then set aside.

In a cool mixing bowl, beat the egg whites until soft peaks form. Add the remaining 2 tablespoons of sugar and beat until the peaks become stiff.

Using the rubber spatula, gradually fold the egg whites into the chestnut paste mixture. Pour this into the caramel-lined baking dish and bake for 35 minutes. Allow to cool and serve directly from the baking dish accompanied by crème anglaise (page 18).

SERVES 8.

RAISIN AND RUM BREAD

½ cup raisins
3 tablespoons rum
½ cup sugar
4 eggs
1 cup flour
1 cup milk
1 teaspoon baking powder
½ cup unsalted, melted butter

Preheat the oven to 350 degrees.

One hour before cooking, marinate the raisins and the rum in a small bowl.

Butter and sugarcoat a 1½ quart baking dish; set aside.

Use a whisk to beat the sugar and the eggs in a large mixing bowl. Sift in the flour and mix. Add the milk, baking powder, and butter; blend well. Strain the raisins and stir them into the batter. Pour the batter into the baking dish. Bake for 25–30 minutes.

Allow the bread to cool before serving. It can be served with crème anglaise (page 18) or crème pâtissière (page 19).

SERVES 8.

CRUNCHY HAZELNUT CAKE

4 eggs
1 cup sugar
1 cup flour
2 tablespoons Pastis liqueur
2 tablespoons heavy cream
1 cup chopped walnuts and hazelnuts mixed

Preheat the oven to 350 degrees.

Use a whisk to beat the eggs and sugar in a large mixing bowl. Sift in the flour and mix. Blend in the Pastis and the heavy cream, then set aside for 10 minutes.

Pour the batter into the baking dish. Sprinkle the top evenly with the nuts. Bake for 30–35 minutes.

Remove the cake from the oven, unmold it, and allow it to cool before before serving topped with your favorite ice cream. This cake can also be sliced and stored in a dry, airtight box for up to 1 week. When completely cooled and properly stored, it becomes crunchy, or *croquant*.

SERVES 8.

CARAMEL PUDDING

½ cup caramel sauce (page 21)
5 eggs
½ cup sugar
1 teaspoon vanilla extract
2 cups milk

Preheat the oven to 350 degrees.

Coat a 1½ quart baking dish with the caramel; set it aside.

Combine the eggs, the sugar, the vanilla extract, and the milk in a mixing bowl. Pour the mixture into the baking dish. Place the dish into a hot bain-marie. Bake for 30 minutes. Set aside to cool, then refrigerate until ready to serve.

SERVES 8.

ROULÉ À LA VANILLE

ROULÉ:
6 eggs
1 cup sugar
¾ cup flour
¼ cup arrowroot

FILLING:
2 cups heavy cream
¼ cup sugar
1 tablespoon vanilla extract

COATING:
6 tablespoons water
1 tablespoon sugar
1 tablespoon vanilla extract
6 tablespoons raspberry sauce
(page 21)

GARNISH:
3 sprigs fresh mint
¼ pound fresh berries
2 tablespoons sweet chocolate powder

Preheat the oven to 350 degrees.

Butter and sugarcoat a 13" × 17", 1" deep non-stick cookie sheet; set aside.

Roulé: Beat the eggs and the sugar in a mixing bowl with an electric beater at a high speed until the mixture turns pale yellow and fluffy.

Sift the flour and the arrowroot into a separate mixing bowl. Little by little, stir the flour mixture into the whipped eggs. Pour the batter onto the cookie sheet; use a spatula to spread it evenly. Bake the roulé for 15 minutes. Remove it from the oven and set it aside to cool.

Filling: In a cool bowl, beat the heavy cream with an electric beater on a high speed until it turns fluffy and peaks form. Use an egg whisk to stir in the ¼ cup of sugar and the vanilla extract. Set aside.

When the roulé has completely cooled, use a sharp, serrated knife to slice it in half horizontally. Store one of the halves in the refrigerator for use in another recipe; place the second half onto a large serving tray; set aside.

Coating: Combine 6 tablespoons of water, the sugar, and the vanilla extract in a cup and mix with a fork. Use a pastry brush to spread the mixture onto the halved roulé. Top evenly with the raspberry sauce. Cover the preserves with a ½" thick layer of the heavy cream mixture. Roll the roulé to form a tube. Cover the top and sides with the remaining cream.

Garnish: Decorate with fresh mint and berries. Sprinkle with the chocolate powder. Refrigerate until ready to serve.

SERVES 8.

RICE CROWN WITH FRESH APRICOTS

1 cup long-grain white rice
3 cups water
4 cups milk
1 vanilla bean, split
1 cup plus 2 teaspoons sugar
6 eggs
6 fresh apricots, washed, dried, pitted, and sliced

Preheat the oven to 400 degrees.

Combine the rice with 3 cups of water in a large saucepan and bring to a boil. Turn heat down and simmer for 10 minutes (the rice should still be crunchy). Rinse the rice in a strainer under cold running water, then pour it back into the saucepan. Add the milk and the vanilla bean and simmer over a medium flame until done, about 45 minutes.

Remove the casserole from the heat and add 1 cup of the sugar and the eggs, whisking after adding each egg.

Butter and sugarcoat a 2 quart mold. Line the bottom of the mold with ⅓ of the apricot slices. Cover them with ½ of the rice mixture. Add ¾ of the remaining apricots. Pour in the balance of the rice mixture up to ½" from the top of the rim. Top with the remaining apricot slices. Sprinkle with the remaining 2 teaspoons of sugar.

Place the mold in a bain-marie and bake for 35 minutes. Cool completely before serving. Unmold onto a serving dish and serve with an apricot sauce (page 23).

SERVES 6–8.

PINEAPPLE CAKE

1½ cup unsalted butter (1 cup melted)
1 cup, plus 7 tablespoons, sugar
4 tablespoons water
1 medium size pineapple, peeled, halved, and cut into ¼" slices
3 entire eggs
3 egg yolks
3 egg whites
1 cup flour
2 tablespoons rum

Preheat the oven to 350 degrees.

Butter and sugarcoat a 9" cake pan; set it aside.

Combine ½ cup of the butter, 6 tablespoons of the sugar, and 4 tablespoons of water in a large casserole over a medium flame. When the mixture begins to darken and caramelize, add the pineapple. Continue to simmer for 3–4 minutes, turning the pineapple slices with a spatula so that both sides are cooked and coated. Drain the pineapple slices in a sieve; set aside.

Mix together 1 cup of the sugar, the eggs, and the egg yolks in a large bowl until well blended. Sift in the flour and blend; stir in the melted butter and the rum. Set aside.

In a cool bowl, beat the remaining tablespoon of sugar and the 3 egg whites with an electric mixer until they become fluffy and stiff. Use a rubber spatula to fold the egg whites into the batter.

Arrange one layer of pineapples around the sides and bottom of the cake pan. Pour in the batter. Bake for 20 minutes. Allow the cake to cool before serving.

SERVES 8.

WHITE CORNMEAL CAKE

2 eggs
1½ cups milk
4 tablespoons heavy cream
1 tablespoon vanilla extract
5 tablespoons unsalted butter, room temperature
2 cups white cornmeal
½ cup flour
6 tablespoons sugar
2 tablespoons baking powder

Preheat the oven to 350 degrees.

Butter and sugarcoat a 1½ quart baking dish; set aside.

In a bowl beat the eggs and the milk in a bowl with an electric mixer. Beat in the heavy cream, the vanilla extract, and the butter. Add the dry ingredients and mix well. Pour the batter into the baking dish. Bake for 20 minutes. Serve warm or cooled.

SERVES 6–8.

WHOLE WHEAT APPLE CAKE

3 entire eggs
3 egg yolks
3 egg whites
1 cup, plus 1 tablespoon, sugar
1 cup whole wheat flour
1 teaspoon baking powder
1 cup margarine, room temperature
1½ cups dried apple slices, diced into ¼" pieces

Preheat the oven to 350 degrees.

Butter and sugarcoat a 9" × 3" springform cake pan; set it aside.

In a medium size bowl mix the 3 eggs, 3 egg yolks, and 1 cup of the sugar with an egg whisk; save the additional 1 tablespoon. Beat in the flour and the baking powder, then the soft margarine. Add the diced apples and blend well; set aside.

In a cool bowl, whip the 3 egg whites with an electric mixer until soft peaks form. Add the remaining tablespoon of sugar and continue to whip until the peaks become stiff. Use a spatula to fold the fluffy egg whites into the batter. Pour the mixture into the cake pan. Bake for 45 minutes. Unmold and cool before serving.

SERVES 8.

WALNUT CAKE

2¼ cups of shelled walnuts
3 slices of white bread
4 egg yolks
4 egg whites
½ cup sugar, plus 2 tablespoons
1 tablespoon of Frangelico or Grand Marnier liqueur

GARNISH:
6 ounces dark, sweet chocolate, chopped

Preheat the oven to 350 degrees.

Butter and sugarcoat a 6" × 3" loaf cake pan; set aside.

Using a food processor, process the nuts for 30 seconds; do not overprocess. Empty into a large mixing bowl. Process the sliced bread into crumbs and add to the nuts. Beat in the egg yolks and ½ cup of the sugar; save the extra 2 tablespoons. Beat in the liqueur; set aside.

Using an electric mixer and a cool bowl, beat the egg whites until soft peaks form. Add the remaining 2 tablespoons of sugar and beat until peaks become stiff.

Fold the stiff egg whites into the nut and bread crumb mixture; pour into the cake pan. Bake for 50 minutes.

Garnish: Melt the chopped chocolate with 2 tablespoons of hot water in a double boiler.

Unmold the cake and turn it upside down. Cover entirely with the melted chocolate. Decorate with a few leftover whole walnuts. This cake can also be served sprinkled with confectioners' sugar, or, for a fancier cake, with a vanilla crème anglaise (page 18).

SERVES 6.

ERIC'S CHOCOLATE CAKE

5 egg yolks
5 egg whites
1²/₃ cups, plus 1 tablespoon, sugar
1 cup finely chopped semisweet chocolate
1 cup flour

Preheat the oven to 350.

Butter and flour a 7" × 3" springform cake pan.

In a large bowl, whisk the egg yolks and the sugar until the mixture becomes creamy and pale yellow; save the additional 1 tablespoon. Stir in the chocolate. Sift in the flour; use a large wooden spoon to blend the thickened mixture. Set aside.

In a separate, cool bowl, beat the egg whites with an electric mixer until soft peaks form. Add 1 tablespoon of sugar and beat until the peaks become stiff. Little by little, fold the egg whites into the chocolate mixture. Pour into the cake pan and bake for 40 minutes.

Cool for 10 minutes before unmolding. Serve warm with crème anglaise (page 18).

SERVES 6.

CARROT TOURTE

1 9½" demi-feuilletage pastry shell, uncooked
2½ cups finely julienned carrots
¼ cup raisins
4 eggs
½ cup sugar
1 teaspoon cinnamon
1 cup heavy cream
zest of 1 lemon
1 10" × 10" × ⅛" thick demi-feuilletage pastry sheet

EGG WASH:
1 egg
2 teaspoons cold water

Preheat the oven to 350 degrees.

Sprinkle the carrots evenly in the pastry shell. Top with the raisins.

Whisk the eggs and the sugar in a bowl. Beat in the cinnamon, the heavy cream, and the lemon zest. Pour the filling into the tart pan.

Roll out the pastry dough on a flat, well-floured surface. Place a 9½" plate on top of it. Use a sharp knife to cut away the excess dough from around the plate. Place the pastry circle on top of the tourte. Seal the tourte by pinching the edges of its shell together with the pastry circle.

Egg Wash: Beat the egg together with 2 tablespoons of cold water. Use a pastry brush to lightly cover the top of the tourte's shell with the egg wash.

Bake for 40 minutes.

Remove the tart pan's sides, leaving the tourte on the bottom of the pan. Cool before serving.

SERVES 8.

VERY LIGHT ALMOND CAKE

1 cup blanched almond nut crumbs
½ cup plus 2 tablespoons sugar
½ cup fine white bread crumbs
4 egg yolks
2 entire eggs
2 tablespoons Amaretto liqueur
4 egg whites
2 tablespoons roasted pine kernels (optional)

Butter and sugarcoat a 9½" cake pan.

Preheat the oven to 300 degrees.

If almond nut crumbs are not readily available at your grocery store, process whole nuts with a food processor or blender. Pour the crumbs into a large bowl. Add ½ cup of the sugar, reserving the additional 2 tablespoons, and the bread crumbs and mix (any plain white bread can be processed into fine crumbs). Beat the egg yolks and the eggs. Add the Amaretto; set aside.

In a separate, cool bowl, beat the egg whites with an electric mixer until soft peaks form. Add 2 tablespoons of sugar, then beat until the peaks become stiff. Fold the egg whites into the mixture. Pour into the cake pan. Sprinkle top with the pine kernels and bake for 30–35 minutes. Unmold and cool before serving.

SERVES 6.

ALMOND MILK PUDDING
(Dessert without Eggs)

>1½ cups milk
>1½ cups almond nut powder, finely ground from whole nuts
>6 tablespoons sugar
>1 tablespoon Amaretto liqueur
>1½ teaspoons unflavored gelatine
>
>SAUCE:
>1 cup milk
>1 tablespoon Amaretto liqueur

Butter 6 2½" × 1½" deep ramekins and set them aside.

Combine the milk, almond nut powder, sugar, and Amaretto in a large saucepan and mix. Bring to a boil over a medium high flame. Remove from the heat immediately and set aside.

Mix the gelatine with the hot mixture. Spoon the liquid into the ramekins. Arrange them on a tray and refrigerate for 5–6 hours. Serve accompanied by the sauce. This light dessert can be made 1 day in advance.

Sauce: Mix the cold milk and the Amaretto. Refrigerate until ready for use.

SERVES 6.

ORANGE SWEETS

1 thick-skinned orange
1 cup hot water
2½ cups sugar
4 ounces bittersweet chocolate, melted

Remove lengthwise 1″ × 1″ sections of orange peel. Cut them into narrow strips and place the strips into a saucepan. Add 1 cup of hot water and 2 cups of sugar; reserve the additional ½ cup. Bring to boil over a medium flame. Reduce the heat and simmer for 15 minutes.

Use a slotted spoon to remove the orange strips from the water; drain on paper towels. Coat half of the strips in the remaining sugar. Place on a serving dish. Coat the balance of the strips in the melted chocolate. Place on the serving dish. Allow to cool before serving.

MAKES ABOUT 24 THIN SLICES.

CHAPTER 4
GRANDMA'S COUNTRY CAKES

YOGURT CAKE

I remember, when I was a little boy, how much I loved the odor of hot yogurt cake freshly unmolded, and how its great aroma filled my grandmother Marguerite's kitchen with joy and visions of delicious treats to come.

1 cup plain yogurt
½ cup sugar
1 cup flour
1 teaspoon baking powder
4 egg yolks
4 egg whites
zest of 1 orange and 1 tablespoon of Grand Marnier for flavoring (optional)

Preheat the oven to 350 degrees.
 Butter and sugarcoat the inside of a 7" × 4" cake mold; set aside.
 Mix the yogurt and sugar in a large bowl. Sift in the flour, then stir in the baking powder, the egg yolks, orange zest, and liqueur with a wooden spoon. Set aside.
 In a separate, cool bowl, beat the egg whites until they are stiff. Gently fold them into the yogurt mixture. Pour the mixture into the mold and bake for 35 minutes. Unmold and serve cooled.

SERVES 6–8.

DIPLOMATE AU POIRE

1 génoise cake (page 20)
6 poached pears (page 24)
4 tablespoons pear brandy
6 eggs
1 cup sugar
1½ cups milk

Preheat the oven to 400 degrees.

Using a sharp knife, trim the bottom and top crust from the génoise cake. Cut the cake in half horizontally; set aside.

Butter a 9" round cake pan; set aside.

Slice the poached pears. Arrange the slices around the bottom of the cake dish so that they overlap slightly; the bottom should be completely covered.

Place one of the halves of the génoise cake over the pears; press down slightly. Sprinkle with 2 tablespoons of the pear brandy. Arrange the remaining pear slices over the génoise cake in a circular design to completely cover it.

Place the second layer of the génoise cake on top of the pear-covered first layer and press down slightly. Sprinkle with the remaining 2 tablespoons of pear brandy. Set aside.

Use a whisk to beat the eggs and sugar in a large bowl. Mix in the milk. Pour ⅔ of the milk mixture over the cake, lifting the edges of the top layer to allow the liquid to saturate the bottom layer. Press the layers together again. Pour the remaining milk mixture over the top of the cake.

Place the cake in a bain-marie and bake for 40 minutes.

Remove from the oven and allow to cool. Unmold the cake, allow to cool, and refrigerate until ready to serve. Serve plain, or with crème anglaise (page 18), or a fruit sauce (pages 21–23). The cake can also be sprinkled with the caramel left over from the poached pears and decorated with mint leaves.

SERVES 6–8.

BREAD PUDDING À L'ORANGE

If you find yourself with dry, hard, leftover bread or cake, you can use it to make a simple bread pudding that's wonderful served alone or with crème anglaise (page 18), sour/whipped cream (page 17), or ice cream.

>20 slices of bread, or cake, sliced ½" thick
>zest of 1 orange
>5 eggs
>½ cup sugar
>1 tablespoon Grand Marnier or Cointreau
>½ clove, crushed
>1½ cups milk

Preheat the oven to 350 degrees.

Butter a 9" baking dish. Cover the bottom of the dish with half of the bread slices. Sprinkle with ¼ of the orange zest.

Use a whisk to beat the eggs and sugar in a bowl. Add the liqueur, the remaining orange zest, clove, and milk, and mix again.

Pour ⅔ of the mixture into the baking dish. Add another layer of bread, then saturate it with the remaining liquid. Place the baking dish in a bain-marie. Bake for 30 minutes.

Remove from the oven and set aside to cool. Serve at room temperature, or refrigerate until ready to serve.

SERVES 4.

COUNTRY POUND CAKE

5 eggs
1 cup sugar
1 cup flour
½ cup unsalted butter, melted
1 teaspoon vanilla extract
1 teaspoon baking powder
1 tablespoon brown sugar (optional)

Preheat the oven to 350 degrees.

Butter and sugarcoat an 8″ cake pan; set aside.

Beat together the eggs and sugar. Sift in the flour and mix well using a whisk. Add the butter, vanilla extract, baking powder. Pour the batter into the pan and bake for 20 minutes. Sprinkle the cake with the brown sugar; then return the cake to the oven and bake 10 minutes more, or until a toothpick stuck into it comes out clean.

Unmold the cake onto a serving dish and serve warm or at room temperature. It can be served plain, or accompanied with a crème anglaise (page 18), or ice cream.

SERVES 8.

LA DOUCEUR DE TANTE ADELE

1 cup water
2 tablespoons sugar
3 tablespoons dark rum
50 1" × 4" ladyfingers (page 26)
1½ cup orange marmalade
1 cup raisins

Preheat the oven to 350 degrees.

Butter and sugarcoat a 7" × 4" charlotte mold; set aside.

In a small bowl, stir together 1 cup of water, the sugar, and the rum. One by one, dip the ladyfingers into the mixture and line the sides of the mold vertically. Line the bottom of the mold with more ladyfingers, and set aside.

Mix the marmalade and raisins in a bowl. Spoon ⅓ of this mixture into the mold. Top with ladyfingers dipped into the rum mixture. Repeat this procedure, finishing with the dipped ladyfingers. Sprinkle with 2 tablespoons of the rum mixture, and place the mold in a bain-marie. Bake for 25–30 minutes.

Remove from the bain-marie and allow to cool 10 minutes before unmolding. Serve with crème anglaise (page 18) flavored with rum.

SERVES 6.

MY GRANDMOTHER'S CHOCOLATE CAKE

This chocolate cake is easy to make, and best of all, it is very light. To enjoy the flavor at its maximum, it should be served at room temperature.

>   *4 ounces bittersweet chocolate*
>   *2 tablespoons water*
>   *½ cup, plus 1 tablespoon, sugar*
>   *½ cup unsalted butter*
>   *¼ cup flour*
>   *3 egg yolks*
>   *3 egg whites*
>   *2 tablespoons roasted pignoli (pine kernels; optional)*
>   *zest of 1 orange (optional)*

Preheat the oven to 350 degrees.

Butter a 9½" cake pan; set aside.

Break the chocolate into small chunks. Over a low flame, melt it in a saucepan with 2 tablespoons of hot water. Stir in the sugar, reserving the additional 1 tablespoon. When completely melted, add the butter, little by little, stirring constantly with a wooden spoon.

Sift in the flour and mix in. Remove from the heat. Add the egg yolks, stirring after each. Set aside to cool.

Beat the egg whites with an electric mixer until soft peaks form. Add 1 tablespoon of sugar and beat until the peaks become stiff. Fold into the batter. Pour into the cake pan. Sprinkle with the nuts and the orange zest. Bake for 20 minutes.

Unmold and set aside to cool. Serve with whipped cream (page 17), or crème anglaise (page 18).

SERVES 8.

SPICE BREAD

½ cup sugar
½ cup dark molasses
¼ cup soft unsalted butter
½ cup boiling water
1 teaspoon baking powder
1 cup unsalted pecans
½ cup raisins
2 eggs, beaten
1 teaspoon ginger powder
¼ teaspoon nutmeg
1 teaspoon cinnamon
1 clove, crushed
¾ cup flour

Preheat the oven to 350 degrees.

Butter and sugarcoat a 5½" × 8" loaf cake pan; set aside.

Mix the sugar, the molasses, the butter, and ½ cup of boiling water in a large saucepan. Stir the mixture over a medium flame until the butter melts. Remove from the heat and stir in the baking powder.

Process the pecans into crumbs. Add to the mixture. Using a whisk, stir in the raisins, the eggs, the ginger, the nutmeg, the cinnamon, and the cloves. Sift in the flour.

Pour the mixture into the pan and bake for 30–40 minutes, or until a toothpick inserted in the center comes out clean. Unmold and set aside to cool.

Cut into 1" slices and serve with whipped cream (page 17).

SERVES 8.

CHERRY CLAFOUTIS

LITTLE PISTACHIO CUPS

ORANGE TART

TULIPS WITH FRESH FRUIT

CHAPTER 5

TARTS

CARAMELIZED APPLE TART

4 large apples, peeled, cored, and quartered
1 tablespoon soft butter
3 tablespoons sugar
1 8" demi-feuilletage pastry shell (page 15) baked in a tart pan with a removable bottom
3 tablespoons apple sauce (page 22)
confectioners' sugar

Preheat the broiler.
    Butter a cookie sheet. Cut the quartered apples into ¼ inch slices. Arrange in rows on the cookie sheet. Dot the butter over the sliced apples. Sprinkle with sugar and broil for 10 minutes, or until the slices turn golden brown.
    Remove the tart pan's sides from the cooked pastry shell leaving the shell on the bottom of the tart pan. Spread the apple sauce evenly over the inside bottom of the shell. Arrange the browned apple slices in a circular design on top of the apple sauce. Sprinkle with confectioners' sugar. Serve warm.

SERVES 4–6.

COUNTRY TART

2 tablespoons sour cream
1 egg
4 tablespoons sugar
pinch of ground nutmeg
1 8" demi-feuilletage pastry shell (page 15)
7 plums or quinces, sliced

Preheat the oven to 400 degrees.

Mix the sour cream, egg, 2 tablespoons of the sugar, and the nutmeg together in a bowl. Pour the mixture into the tart shell. Arrange the sliced fruit in a circular design on the bottom of the pastry shell. Sprinkle with the remaining 2 tablespoons of sugar and bake for 30 minutes. Serve warm.

SERVES 6.

RHUBARB TART

1 9" demi-feuilletage pastry shell, uncooked (page 15)
½ pound rhubarb, stems peeled and cut into ½" cubes
4 tablespoons sugar
1½ tablespoons soft, unsalted butter

Preheat the oven to 350 degrees.

Fill the unbaked pastry shell with the diced rhubarb. Sprinkle with the sugar. Dot the butter evenly over the tart. Bake for 40 minutes. Serve warm.

While one of the simplest tarts to make, this is also one of the tastiest.

SERVES 6.

CHOCOLATE AND PINE KERNEL TART

4 ounces semisweet, dark chocolate, chopped
1 8" demi-feuilletage (page 15) or pâté brisée pastry shell (page 16)
2 ounces pignoli (pine kernels)
zest of 1 orange
3 eggs
½ cup sugar
1 tablespoon Grand Marnier (optional)
¾ cup heavy cream

GARNISH:
zest of 1 orange
½ cup hot water
4 tablespoons sugar
1 tablespoon water
sprig of fresh mint

Preheat the oven to 400 degrees.

Sprinkle the chopped chocolate evenly over the pastry shell. Sprinkle in the nuts.

Beat the zest, eggs, sugar, and Grand Marnier in a bowl. Blend in the heavy cream. Pour the mixture into the tart shell. Bake for 30 minutes.

Garnish: Using a vegetable peeler, peel thin pieces of zest off the orange. Place the zest, ½ cup of hot water, and the sugar into a saucepan and bring to a boil. Continue boiling for 15 minutes until the liquid is reduced to a slightly thick syrup. Set aside.

Remove the tart pan's sides from around the tart. Remove the orange zest strips from the syrup and arrange them in a pretty design on top of the tart.

Add 1 tablespoon of water to the syrup and reheat it for 1 minute. Drizzle the syrup over the top of the tart to glaze it. Garnish the tart with the fresh mint.

SERVES 4–6.

TARTE TATIN

½ cup unsalted butter
1 cup sugar
1 cup water
½ teaspoon vanilla extract
5 large red Rome apples, peeled, cored, and sliced
  ½" thick
1 9" × 9" sheet of pâte brisée pastry (page 16)

Preheat the oven to 400 degrees.

Butter and sugarcoat an 8½" Teflon-coated skillet; set aside.

Combine the butter, sugar, water, and vanilla extract in an 8½" heavy skillet. Over a high flame, boil until the ingredients caramelize, stirring occasionally to prevent sticking. When the mixture becomes completely brown, add the apples and cook until just done.

Meanwhile, roll out a thin layer of the pâte brisée. Using a plate the same size as the skillet, cut out a round circle of the pastry.

When the apples are done, drain them in a sieve. Using a fork, arrange the apple slices in a circle around the bottom and sides of the skillet. Add the rest of the apples and press down on them with a fork so that they are evenly distributed. Place the skillet over a high flame; bring any remaining liquid just to a boil, then remove from the heat. Lay the pastry sheet over the top of the apples. Bake for 15–20 minutes, then remove from the oven.

Being careful not to burn yourself with the hot skillet, place a large serving plate over the skillet and turn the tarte out onto the plate. Serve hot or cold with whipped sour cream (page 17).

SERVES 4–6.

LEMON TART

1 cup freshly squeezed lemon juice
¾ cup unsalted butter
zest of 3 lemons
1 cup sugar
5 entire eggs
1 9½" demi-feuilletage pastry shell (page 15), cooked
1 cup egg whites, about 6 egg whites

Stir together the lemon juice, butter, lemon zest, and ½ cup of sugar in a medium size saucepan. Bring to a boil over a high flame for 2 minutes.

In another medium size saucepan, beat the eggs with an egg whisk. Little by little, whisking constantly, beat the hot mixture into the eggs. Return to the heat, stirring constantly to prevent sticking. Do not allow to boil. As it thickens, test for readiness by dipping a wooden spoon into the sauce and running your finger across the back of the spoon. If the sauce runs back into the finger trace, it needs more cooking. If the finger trace stays clean, it has cooked enough.

Pour the custard into the shell. Allow to cool completely, then refrigerate for 20 minutes.

Preheat the broiler.

In a cool bowl, beat together the remaining ½ cup of sugar with the egg whites until stiff peaks form. Using a flat spatula or a knife, spread the meringue decoratively on top of the tart. Place under the broiler just until the meringue turns golden brown. Allow to cool before serving.

SERVES 6.

TEA TART SHELLS

pâte brisée or demi-feuilletage pastry dough (pages 16 and 15)

Preheat the oven to 350 degrees.

Roll out a thin 16" circle of pastry dough on a floured work space. Butter 10–12 (depending on size) small, individual tart tins (about 2"–4") of different sizes and shapes; set them aside.

Use a round cookie cutter to cut out pastry circles slightly larger than the tart tins. Place a circle over each, then gently fit the dough into the tins. Use a fork to punch holes in the bottom of the larger pastry shells. Fit the larger of the tart tins with small squares of aluminum foil, then fill them with rice or beans to weigh them. The small shells do not need weights, but some can be stacked into each other, placed in the oven and baked for 10–15 minutes. Place the remaining small tins on a buttered cookie sheet and bake until golden brown, about 10–15 minutes. Remove all of the baked shells from the oven and set them aside to cool.

Butter another large cookie sheet. Cut out twelve 2" circles of pastry. Place them on the cookie sheet; cover the pastry circles with a sheet of foil. Weigh the dough with rice or beans, then bake for 35 minutes. Remove from the oven and set aside to cool.

Remove the weights and foil from the tart shells that have cooled. Bake again for 15 minutes (they must be baked until completely cooked and dry).

Use a 3" cookie cutter to cut out 8 pastry circles. Fit the circles into 2" round tart tins. Place on a buttered cookie sheet and bake for 10–15 minutes; set aside to cool.

Roll out a 12" circle of the pastry dough, about ½" thick. Use a 1½" round cookie cutter to cut out circles. Fit them into 2" cookie tins and bake for 10–15 minutes; set aside to cool. These shells will later be cut in half horizontally and filled. Accordingly, they are thicker than the previous shells.

FILLINGS FOR TEA TART SHELLS

Apple Filling for Tart Shells

2 tablespoons unsalted butter
3 tablespoons sugar
3 tablespoons water
2 apples, peeled, cored, and diced

All of the shells must be very dry so they will remain crisp when garnished or filled.

Combine the butter, the sugar, and 3 tablespoons of water in a saucepan and place it over a medium flame. Stir occasionally, cooking until the ingredients caramelize. Place the diced apples into the caramel and stir to coat them. Continue to cook 2 minutes more.

Use a slotted spoon to remove the diced apples, then purée them in a food processor. Set aside to cool, then refrigerate until purée becomes cold.

Nectarine Tart Filling

4 nectarines or peaches, peeled, pitted, and diced
8 tablespoons water

Combine the fruit and 8 tablespoons of water in a saucepan. Cook over a medium flame for 15 minutes. Remove from the heat and set aside to cool.

Orange Filling

2 oranges, cut into thin slices
4 tablespoons sugar
8 tablespoons water

Combine the oranges, sugar, and 8 tablespoons of water in a saucepan. Cook over a medium flame for 15 minutes. Remove from the heat and set aside to cool.

FILLING FOR TART CIRCLES

¼ cup crème pâtissière (page 19)
2 kiwifruits, peeled and thinly sliced
3 prunes, thinly sliced
1 very ripe pear, peeled and sliced thinly
½ tablespoon sugar
½ tablespoon butter, room temperature
½ pound fresh blueberries
½ pound fresh strawberries, sliced, or small raspberries
½ cup whipped cream (page 17)

GARNISHES
½ cup whipped cream (page 17)
6 violet petals (crystallized variety found in fine food shops)
16 rose petals (crystallized variety found in fine food shops)
1 bunch fresh mint
zest of 1 lemon

Spread the flat, round, tart circles with crème pâtissière. Top some with the kiwi slices, others with the prune slices, and the remaining tart circles with the pear slices. Sprinkle with the sugar and top each with a dot of butter. Place under the broiler to melt the butter and the sugar. Set aside to cool.

Meanwhile, cut the thicker 1½" pastry circles in half horizontally. Bake again until they are absolutely dry in the center, about 10 minutes. Set aside to cool. When cooled, fill with the remaining crème pâtissière. Top some with the fresh blueberries, others with fresh, sliced strawberries, or small raspberries.

Spoon the cooled, diced nectarine or peach into some of the small tart shells.

Remove the apple purée from the refrigerator. Spoon onto the remaining thick 1½" rounds that have been cut in half horizontally. Top each with ¼ teaspoon of whipped cream. Cover with the top half of the shell. Sprinkle with confectioners' sugar.

Arrange all of the tarts on a large serving tray. Garnish the prune tarts with crystallized violet petal candies; the orange tarts with crystallized rose candies and 1 fresh mint leaf; the pear tarts with 1 raspberry and 1 mint leaf each; the strawberry and blueberry tarts with the lemon zest; the apple purée tarts with 1 raspberry and 1 mint leaf each.

ORANGE TART

zest of 2 oranges
4 tablespoons fresh squeezed orange juice
⅓ cup melted, unsalted butter
2 tablespoons Grand Marnier
3 eggs
1 11" cooked pâte brisée pie shell (page 16)
¾ cup sugar
2 large, seedless oranges, thinly sliced
1 cup water

Preheat the oven to 350 degrees.

Combine the zest, juice, butter, and Grand Marnier in a bowl and blend well.

In a separate bowl, combine the eggs and ¼ cup of the sugar until the mixture becomes light and fluffy. Slowly add the orange juice mixture, beating well. Pour the mixture into the pie shell and bake for 40 minutes. Remove from the oven and set aside.

Bring the orange slices, the remaining ½ cup of sugar, and 1 cup of water to a boil in a large saucepan. Simmer until the orange slices are cooked, about 20 minutes. Remove the slices from the liquid with a slotted spoon; reserve the liquid in the saucepan.

Cut the orange slices in half and, starting in the center of the pastry shell, arrange them in a circle overlapping the edges. Place the remaining slices around the edge of the tart.

Reduce the reserved liquid to a syrup over high heat and pour over the tart as a glaze. Serve hot, or, if preferred, at room temperature.

SERVES 8.

CINNAMON APPLE PUDDING
(Cake without Eggs)

1 pound Granny Smith Apples, peeled, cored, and diced into ½" cubes
2 tablespoons fresh lemon juice
1 pound loaf of white bread, sliced
zest of 1 lemon
1½ cup pure apple juice
½ cup soft raisins (not too dry)
½ cup sugar
2 tablespoons cinnamon

Preheat the oven to 350.

Butter and sugarcoat a 7" × 4" soufflé mold; set aside.

Sprinkle the diced apples with the lemon juice and set aside.

Remove the crust from the bread slices and mix with the lemon zest and the apple juice in a large bowl, gently breaking the bread into smaller pieces with a wooden spoon. Blend in the raisins. Pour a ½" layer of this filling mixture into the mold. Top with a layer of the apples.

Combine the sugar and cinnamon in a cup. Sprinkle 2 tablespoons of this mixture over the apples. Repeat these layering steps of filling, apples, sugar–cinnamon mixture until all of the ingredients are used, finishing with the cinnamon–sugar mixture. Bake for 25–30 minutes.

This dessert should be cooked in a pretty mold and served from it. Allow to cool first, and accompany with sour or whipped cream (page 17).

SERVES 6.

CHAPTER 6
DESSERTS MADE WITH FRESH FRUITS AND VEGETABLES

POTATO AND APRICOT PANNEQUET

1½ pounds white potatoes, peeled, diced into large chunks
3 ounces dried apricots
1 cup water
4 tablespoons rum
½ cup soft, unsalted butter
¼ teaspoon salt
3 eggs
2 tablespoons sugar
2 tablespoons honey
2 tablespoons sour cream
zest of 1 orange
2 tablespoons brown sugar

Preheat the oven to 350 degrees.

Boil the diced potatoes until done, about 15 minutes. Soften the apricots in 1 cup of water for 2–3 minutes; set aside.

Mash the cooked potatoes in a large bowl. Add the apricots, the rum, the butter, and the salt and mix well, using a rubber spatula.

Beat the eggs in a separate bowl and blend gently into the potato mixture. Mix in the sugar, the honey, the sour cream, and the orange zest.

Butter the sides and bottom of a heavy 10″ skillet. Heat the skillet until very hot; do not allow the butter to burn. Pour the potato mixture into the skillet and cook over a medium high flame for 1 minute. Sprinkle with the brown sugar. Place the skillet into the hot oven and bake for 15 minutes. Allow to cool, then serve with a raspberry sauce (page 21).

SERVES 6.

PLANTAIN FRITTERS

4 large, green plantains, peeled
½ cup peanut oil
3 eggs
1 cup sugar
2 tablespoons dark rum

COATING:
1 cup peanut oil
2 eggs, beaten
1 cup sugar
zest of 1 lime

Cut each plantain into thirds. Heat the oil in a large skillet; sauté the plantains until browned on all sides, about 10 minutes, turning them often with a long handled fork or a pair of tongs. Remove the cooked plantain slices from the oil and drain them on paper towels.

Place the slices in the bowl of a food processor and coarsely process. Add the eggs and the sugar and process the mixture again until it is smooth but not too creamy, about 30 seconds. Pour the mixture into a bowl and blend in the rum using a rubber spatula.

Using a soup spoon, scoop out enough of the mixture to form a small ball. Set it on a large plate. Repeat this step until all of the mixture has been used.

Heat the oil in a large skillet. Use your hands to flatten the balls into ¼" patties, then dip them into the beaten egg and place them in the hot oil. Brown about 1 minute on each side.

Remove the patties from the oil and drain them on paper towels. Dip each patty into the sugar to coat it. Grate the lime zest over them and serve immediately.

These little fritters are wonderful served with cheese as an afternoon tea snack.

SERVES 4.

CHOCOLATE POTATO CAKE

2 pounds large white potatoes, peeled, washed, and diced
saucepan of water
8 ounces semisweet chocolate
½ cup soft, unsalted butter
½ teaspoon baking powder
¼ teaspoon salt
3½ tablespoons sugar
5 egg yolks
zest of 1 orange
5 egg whites
1 tablespoon confectioners' sugar

Preheat the oven to 350 degrees.

Butter and sugarcoat an 8½" × 3" loaf cake pan; set aside.

Place the diced potatoes into a medium size saucepan filled with water. Bring to a boil and cook until done, about 20–25 minutes.

Meanwhile, melt the chocolate in a bain-marie in the preheated oven.

Drain the potatoes in a colander and place them into a mixing bowl. Add the butter. Mash the potatoes by hand with a potato masher or a fork.

In another mixing bowl, mix together the melted chocolate and baking powder. Add the salt, 2 tablespoons of the sugar, and the egg yolks, 1 at a time, beating the mixture after adding each yolk. Add the zest.

Beat the egg whites until they form soft peaks. Add the remaining 1½ tablespoons of sugar and continue to beat until the peaks are stiff. Slowly fold the egg whites into the potato–chocolate mixture. Pour the mixture into the cake pan, place it in the hot oven, and bake for 45 minutes.

Remove from the oven, sprinkle with the confectioners' sugar; set aside to cool. Serve with crème anglaise (recipe page 18) or with whipped sour cream (recipe page 17).

SERVES 8.

PETITES FLORENTINES PARMENTIER

Once the most underappreciated vegetable in France, the potato won acceptance for its nutritive value through the strong support of Antoine Augustine Parmentier, an eighteenth century pharmacist and agronomist. Today it is used in dishes from soup to omelettes to desserts. The recipe that follows is simple to make, yet distinctly different. It's moist and light in texture, and makes a perfect snack for kids and grownups alike.

12 small red potatoes, peeled and julienned
1 egg, beaten
¼ teaspoon cinnamon
¼ teaspoon salt
1 tablespoon sugar
2 tablespoons peanut oil

Preheat the oven to 350 degrees.

Stir the julienned potatoes into the beaten egg until completely coated. Add the cinnamon, salt, and sugar; mix thoroughly.

Heat the oil in a heavy skillet. Into the oil, using a fork, spread a thin layer about 3" wide of the mixture to make each florentine. Cook about 2 minutes on each side, or until golden. Remove with a spatula and drain on a platter covered with paper towels. Serve hot with a glass of buttermilk, or with tea or coffee.

SERVES 6.

SWEET POTATO GRATIN

2 cups milk
1½ pounds sweet potatoes, peeled, diced
3 cloves, crushed
¼ teaspoon cinnamon
zest of 1 lemon
2 tablespoons sugar
⅛ teaspoon allspice
zest of 1 lime
2 eggs
¼ cup Nilla wafer crumbs
1 tablespoon soft, unsalted butter

Preheat the oven to 350 degrees.

Butter and sugarcoat a 9" × 5" × 2½" loaf cake pan; set aside.

Combine the milk and potatoes in a large casserole. Bring to a boil over a medium flame. Add the cloves, cinnamon, lemon zest, sugar, allspice, and lime zest. Simmer for 15 minutes. Pour the mixture into the bowl of a processor; add the eggs and process until smooth, about 30 seconds.

Pour the mixture into the cake pan. Sprinkle with the cookie crumbs and dot the butter evenly over the top of the gratin. Bake for 20 minutes. Allow to cool before serving.

SERVES 4.

TOMATO TOURTE

4½ tablespoons unsalted butter
3 pounds unripe tomatoes, sliced, seeded
skin of 1 lemon, julienned
5 tablespoons water
6 tablespoons sugar
1 egg
1 tablespoon arrowroot
1 9" demi-feuilletage pastry shell, cooked (page 15)

TOPPING:
3 egg whites
2 tablespoons sugar
zest of 1 lemon
peel of 1 tomato
1 tablespoon confectioners' sugar

Melt the butter in a large pan over a medium flame. Add the tomato slices and stir occasionally, being careful not to break the slices.

Meanwhile, place the lemon julienne into a small casserole. Add 5 tablespoons of water and 3 tablespoons of the sugar. Place over a high heat and bring to a boil. Continue to boil until most of the water has evaporated, then strain the lemon julienne and set aside.

Add the remaining 3 tablespoons of sugar to the now cooked tomatoes and stir gently.

Beat together the egg and the arrowroot, then add to the tomato mixture. Remove from the heat and stir in the lemon zest. Pour the mixture into the pastry shell; set aside to cool.

Topping: Preheat the oven to 400 degrees.

Beat the egg whites until soft peaks form. Add the sugar and beat until the peaks are stiff. Add the lemon zest and beat 10 seconds more. Spread the meringue evenly over the cooled tart, using a flat spatula or a knife to create a design. Bake about 5 minutes in the oven, just until the topping is lightly browned.

Using a sharp paring knife, remove the skin from a tomato and curl to form a rose. Sprinkle the tart with the confectioners' sugar. Place the rose in the center of the tart and serve immediately.

SERVES 6.

FRUIT CLAFOUTIS

½ pear, peeled, cored, and finely sliced
½ apple, peeled, cored, and finely sliced
1 plum, pitted and finely sliced
1 peach, peeled, pitted, and cut into thin slices
3 tablespoons raspberries
3 tablespoons blueberries
3 strawberries, halved and sliced
4 eggs
⅔ cups sugar
⅔ cups flour
½ teaspoon baking powder
1 tablespoon Kirsch or eau-de-vie (optional)
1 cup milk
½ cup melted, unsalted butter

Preheat the oven to 350 degrees.

Butter and sugarcoat a 9" cake pan. Place the fruit into the pan and set aside.

Mix the eggs and sugar; sift the flour into the egg mixture and blend. Beat in the baking powder, eau-de-vie, milk, and butter. Pour the mixture over the fruit and bake for 30 minutes. Allow to cool before serving.

SERVES 6.

APPLE BEIGNETS

*4 large Rome apples, cored, peeled, and sliced into
½" -thick rounds
3 tablespoons rum
4 tablespoons sugar
beignet mixture (page 25)
4 cups peanut oil*

Place the apple rounds into a large mixing bowl. Sprinkle them with the rum and 3 tablespoons of the sugar; set aside to marinate for 30 minutes.

Half fill a large skillet with the 4 cups of peanut oil and heat it over a high flame until it is very hot. Dip the apple slices into the beignet mixture. Using tongs, place them, one by one, into the hot oil. Use the tongs to keep the beignets separated and to turn them after about 2 minutes. Cook until golden on both sides, no more than 5 minutes.

Remove from the oil and drain on paper towels. Sprinkle lightly with the remaining tablespoon of sugar. Serve warm or cool, alone or accompanied by a raspberry sauce (page 21) or apple sauce (page 22).

SERVES 6.

MOLLIE'S PEACH COBBLER

demi-feuilletage dough (page 15)
4 ripe peaches, peeled, pitted, and thinly sliced
1½ tablespoons sugar
1 teaspoon cinnamon
1 teaspoon nutmeg
1 teaspoon vanilla extract
3 tablespoons soft, unsalted butter

Preheat the oven to 350 degrees.

Roll out the dough to ⅛" thickness. Cut out enough of the dough to fit the baking dish, crimping the edges along the rim. Set the dish on top of the remaining dough. Use a sharp knife to cut around the bottom's edge to make a pastry sheet. Cut out a second pastry sheet and set both aside.

Spread 2 layers of peach slices in the bottom of the pie shell. Sprinkle with ½ tablespoon of sugar, ½ teaspoon of cinnamon, ½ teaspoon of nutmeg, and ½ teaspoon of vanilla extract. Dot with ½ tablespoon of butter.

Cover with a pastry circle. Repeat the steps in the previous paragraph, then cover with the second pastry sheet. Dot with ½ tablespoon of butter. Sprinkle with ½ tablespoon of sugar.

Bake for 45 minutes. Cooking the cobbler slowly allows the peach juice, sugar, and spices to melt into a delicious caramel. It also allows the crust to cook thoroughly without becoming dry, and to become crispy and golden brown. Cool 15 minutes, then serve with vanilla ice cream.

SERVES 4.

POTATO AND APRICOT GRATIN

¼ pound dried apricots
3 tablespoons rum
1 cup warm water
2 pounds white potatoes, peeled, boiled
½ cup soft, unsalted butter
¼ teaspoon salt
3 eggs
2 tablespoons sugar
2 tablespoons sour cream
2 tablespoons brown sugar

Preheat the oven to 400 degrees.

One hour before cooking, soak the apricots in a mixture of 2 tablespoons of rum and 1 cup of warm water. They should be completely submerged in the liquid.

Mash the cooked potatoes in a large mixing bowl with a fork. Add the apricots, the remaining 1 tablespoon of rum, and the butter. Mix well, using a rubber spatula. Add the salt.

Beat the eggs in a separate bowl and fold into the potato mixture. Mix in the sugar and the sour cream.

Butter and sugarcoat a 1½ quart baking dish; pour the mixture into the baking dish. Sift the brown sugar over the top, then place the dish in a bain-marie. Bake for 30 minutes. Allow to cool, then serve with a glass of buttermilk.

SERVES 6.

RUTH'S BANANA PUDDING

¾ cup sugar
½ cup corn starch
⅛ teaspoon salt
5 egg yolks
2 cups milk
1 vanilla bean, split and scraped out
1 box Nilla wafers
4–6 large, ripe bananas
5 egg whites

Combine ½ cup of the sugar, the corn starch, and the salt in a double boiler (the water in the bottom half of the double boiler should be boiling). Stir in the egg yolks, the milk, and the pulp of the vanilla bean. Continue to cook, stirring constantly until the mixture thickens, about 10–15 minutes.

Meanwhile, place the contents of half of the box of wafers on a hard work surface. Using a rolling pin or a bottle, roll over the wafers to press them into fine crumbs. Spread the crumbs about ¼" thick over the bottom of a 1½ quart casserole. Line the sides of the casserole to its top with some of the wafers.

Thinly slice 2 layers of banana into the casserole and spread them evenly over the bottom of the dish. Cover completely with ¼ of the custard. Slice another 2 layers of banana into the pudding, and again, top with the custard. Repeat these steps until the casserole is filled, finishing with the custard. Set aside.

Turn on the broiler.

In a cool bowl, beat the egg whites until soft peaks form; add the remaining ¼ cup of sugar and continue beating until the peaks are stiff. Spread the mixture on top of the pudding, using a spoon to form a design.

Place the pudding beneath the broiler to brown the meringue, about 2 minutes, or just until the topping is dark gold. Cool before serving.

SERVES 6.

ORANGE BAVAROISE

1 ladyfinger belt (page 26)
1 seedless orange, thinly sliced
1¾ cup sugar
1 cup water
3 cups milk
1 vanilla bean, split
5 egg yolks
3 teaspoons unflavored gelatine
1 teaspoon Grand Marnier
zest of 1 orange

Butter a 8" × 4" cake pan; set aside.

Use a sharp, serrated knife to slice the ladyfinger belt into 3 even layers. Line the sides of the cake pan; set aside.

Combine the orange slices, ¾ cup of sugar, and 1 cup of water in a saucepan. Simmer for 5 minutes over a medium flame.

Bring to a boil the milk and the vanilla bean in a large saucepan. Lower the heat and simmer for 5 minutes.

Use a slotted spoon to remove the orange slices from the hot water. Line the bottom of the cake pan with 1 layer of orange slices. Set aside. Refrigerate the remaining orange slices and use for garnish later.

Whisk the egg yolks and 1 cup of sugar in a saucepan until the mixture becomes pale yellow. Remove the boiling milk from the heat. Slowly add it to the egg yolk mixture. Return to the heat for 2 minutes, stirring continuously to prevent sticking; do not overcook.

Pour the egg yolk mixture through a fine sieve into a large bowl. Whisk in the gelatine, the Grand Marnier, and the orange zest. Pour the mixture into the cake pan over the orange slices. Set aside to cool to room temperature. Refrigerate for 2–3 hours before serving. Top with the leftover orange slices.

SERVES 6.

CHAPTER 7

CRÊPES AND SOUFFLÉS

CRÊPES

4 eggs
1 cup flour
1 cup milk
1 tablespoon peanut oil
¼ teaspoon salt
1 tablespoon unsalted butter (or peanut oil)
1 tablespoon sugar

Beat the eggs with a whisk. Sift in the flour and mix; then the milk. Beat in the peanut oil and the salt. Set the batter aside for 15 minutes before using it.

Heat the butter in a small heavy-bottomed skillet or a crêpe pan. Spread a thin, even layer (about 2 tablespoons) of the batter in the pan. Sprinkle lightly with some of the sugar. Use a spatula to fold the edges of the crêpe, then lift it from the skillet. Serve while hot.

Different garnishes such as jams, marmalades, or almond butter can be used for this light, delicious crêpe. My favorite is a dab of butter sprinkled with brown sugar.

MAKES ABOUT 12 CRÊPES.

CRÊPES MADE WITH WATER

This crêpe batter is especially good for those persons allergic to milk, or who simply dislike using it. It can be refrigerated and stored for up to 2 days. If it becomes too thick, simply add a little water to the batter.

3 eggs
1½ cups whole wheat flour
1½ cups water
½ cup melted, unsalted butter
⅛ teaspoon salt
1 tablespoon unsalted butter (or peanut oil)

Mix the eggs, the flour, and 1½ cups of water in a mixing bowl. Beat in the melted butter and the salt. Set aside for 15 minutes.

Heat the oil in a crêpe pan or a heavy-bottomed skillet. Spread a thin layer of the batter, about 2 tablespoons, in the pan. Cook 30–40 seconds, turn and cook the second side until lightly browned.

Place your choice of garnish, i.e., apple sauce, dried fruit purée, or fresh fruit with cottage cheese, into the center of the crêpe. Fold the edges over and serve it immediately. Another favorite treat of mine is to place an egg into the center of the crêpe after you've turned it. Salt and pepper the egg, and continue to cook the crêpe about 2 minutes, just until the egg is almost done. Fold the edges over and serve it immediately.

MAKES 12 CRÊPES.

CRÊPE À L'ORANGE

3 tablespoons unsalted butter
3 tablespoons sugar
zest of 1 orange
3 tablespoons Grand Marnier
12 crêpes (page 89)

Blend the butter, sugar, orange zest, and Grand Marnier together in a small saucepan over low heat. Sprinkle the sauce over the crêpes and serve immediately.

SERVES 4.

CRÊPE SOUFFLÉ

12 crêpes (page 89)
¼ cup crème pâtissière (page 19)

Preheat the oven to 350 degrees.

Place the hot crêpes on a large platter. Spread 2 teaspoons of the crème pâtissière in the center of each crêpe. Roll the crêpes into small tubes and place on a Teflon-coated cookie sheet. Bake for 12–15 minutes. Serve with crème anglaise (page 18).

SERVES 6.

BASIC SOUFFLÉ MIXTURE

1 tablespoon hot water
3 cups milk
1 vanilla bean, split
6 egg yolks
1 cup sugar
1 cup flour
1 teaspoon baking powder

Preheat the oven to 350 degrees.

In a large saucepan, simmer 1 tablespoon of hot water, the milk, and the vanilla bean over a medium flame.

Use a whisk to beat the egg yolks and the sugar in a large bowl. Sift in the flour and baking powder and mix well. Slowly add the hot milk mixture to the flour–egg yolk mixture while stirring constantly. Pour the mixture into a large, clean saucepan and return it to the heat. Stir continuously until mixture thickens to a paste.

Using a rubber spatula, force the mixture through a fine sieve into a mixing bowl; set aside while preparing the rest of the soufflé.

MAKES 1½ CUPS.

SOUFFLÉ WITH FRESH THYME

In a home kitchen, individual soufflés are easier to prepare because the cooking process is easier to control. Using the basic soufflé recipe on page 92, you can create a delightful variety simply by changing the flavorings. Soufflés made with berries can be served with a sauce made from the same berry; the other soufflés can be served with a crème anglaise (page 18), or your choice of fruit sauce (pages 21–23).

1 tablespoon Strega liqueur or 2 tablespoons B & B
1 teaspoon fresh thyme
1½ cups basic soufflé mixture (page 92)
4 egg whites
2 tablespoons sugar

Preheat the oven to 350 degrees.

Add the liqueur and thyme to the basic soufflé mixture; stir with a rubber spatula.

In a cool bowl, beat the egg whites with an electric mixer on high speed until they form soft peaks. Add the sugar and beat until the peaks become stiff. Slowly fold the egg whites into the basic soufflé mixture; set aside.

Butter and sugarcoat 4 individual 4″ ramekins or soufflé dishes. Fill each with the mixture. Bake for 20 minutes. Serve immediately.

SERVES 4.

FRUIT SOUFFLÉS

RASPBERRY SOUFFLÉ
1½ cups basic soufflé mixture (page 92)
3 tablespoons raspberries, mashed
1 teaspoon raspberry liqueur or alcohol
5 egg whites
2 tablespoons sugar

PETALS DES ROSES
1½ cups basic soufflé mixture (page 92)
12 fragrant rose petals
¼ teaspoon eau-de-rose
5 egg whites
2 tablespoons sugar

LEMON SOUFFLÉ
1½ cups basic soufflé mixture (page 92)
zest of 1 lemon
¼ teaspoon lemon extract
5 egg whites
2 tablespoons sugar

For these soufflés, first preheat the oven to 350 degrees. Add the fruit or flavoring ingredients to the basic soufflé mixture and blend well; set aside.

In a cool bowl, beat the egg whites until they form soft peaks. Add the 2 tablespoons of sugar and beat until the peaks become stiff. Slowly fold the egg whites into the basic soufflé mixture; set aside.

Butter and sugarcoat 4 individual 4″ ramekins or soufflé dishes. Fill each with the mixture. Place in the heated oven for 20 minutes. Serve immediately.

SERVES 4.

FROZEN FRUIT SOUFFLÉ

This frozen soufflé is a perfect zesty, refreshing summer dessert that can be made in a few minutes, requires no cooking, and can be prepared in advance. Besides berries, fresh, diced pineapple can be used, as well as lemon, lime, and orange zest.

1 cup heavy cream
7 tablespoons sugar
1 cup raspberries, or 10 strawberries, mashed
4 egg whites
1 teaspoon fresh lemon juice

Butter and sugarcoat four 4" ramekins or soufflé dishes; set aside. Butter four 3½" wide strips of wax paper. Wrap one of them around each of the ramekins, forming a margin about 1" above each ramekin; keep in place with a rubber band; set aside.

Beat the heavy cream with an electric mixer, at high speed, until the cream thickens. Add 3 tablespoons of sugar and continue to beat. Blend in the mashed berries.

In a cool bowl, beat the egg whites until soft peaks form. Add the remaining 4 tablespoons of sugar and continue to beat until the peaks become stiff. Slowly fold the egg whites into the heavy cream mixture; blend in the lemon juice.

Fill the ramekins to the top of the wax paper. Shake the dish gently to ensure that the mixture is well settled. Use a spoon to smooth the top of the mixture. Freeze for 3–4 hours. Remove the rubber band and paper before serving.

SERVES 4.

OMELETTE SOUFFLÉ

½ cup, plus 2 tablespoons, sugar
1 teaspoon vanilla extract
1 teaspoon rum
3 egg yolks
6 egg whites
⅛ teaspoon salt
1 tablespoon orange zest
½ tablespoon confectioners' sugar

Preheat the oven to 350 degrees.

Butter and sugarcoat a 1½ quart baking dish; set aside.

Whisk together the sugar, reserving the extra 2 tablespoons, the vanilla extract, and the rum in a mixing bowl. Mix in 3 of the egg yolks and set aside.

Place the 6 egg whites into a mixing bowl and beat them with an electric mixer until soft peaks form. Add the remaining 2 tablespoons of sugar and the salt. Beat until the peaks become stiff; set aside.

Stir the orange zest into the egg yolk mixture.

Using a rubber spatula, little by little, gently fold the stiff egg whites into the egg yolk mixture. Do not overblend. Fold evenly into the baking dish. Use a knife to cut several lines through the mixture. (This helps the heat to pass completely through the soufflé.) Bake for 50 minutes. Sprinkle with confectioners' sugar and serve immediately.

SERVES 8.

PINEAPPLE CRÉPINETTE

4 tablespoons sugar
2 tablespoons, plus ½ teaspoon, unsalted butter
1 medium pineapple, peeled, cut in ¼" thick slices
10 crêpes (page 89), of same size as baking dish
zest of 1 orange
1 tablespoon Grand Marnier

Butter and sugarcoat a 7" × 3" baking dish; set aside.

Over a medium flame, melt 4 tablespoons of the sugar with 2 tablespoons of butter in a large skillet. Add the pineapple slices, turning each to coat them. Cook until soft and caramelized, about 10–12 minutes.

Place a crêpe in the bottom of the baking dish. Cover with some of the pineapple slices. Drizzle with 1 tablespoon of the caramel. Sprinkle with ½ teaspoon of orange zest. Cover with a crêpe and repeat the following steps 8 times, finishing with a crêpe. Dot the crêpe with ½ teaspoon of butter. Sprinkle with ½ teaspoon of orange zest and the Grand Marnier.

Place in a hot bain-marie and bake for 30 minutes. Cool before serving.

This dessert should be baked in a pretty dish and served directly from it.

SERVES 4.

CHAPTER 8
BREAKFAST AND COFFEE BREAK

BLUEBERRY MUFFINS

This recipe is so quick and easy that you can pop it into the oven before taking a shower and serve the muffins hot for breakfast 30 minutes later. Raspberries, fresh cranberries, raisins, or dried, chopped apricots make delicious toppings. Peeled, cored, and diced apples with ¼ teaspoon of cinnamon instead of the vanilla extract is also a delicious alternative.

> 3 eggs
> ½ cup sugar
> ½ cup flour
> ¼ teaspoon baking powder
> ½ cup melted, unsalted butter
> ½ teaspoon vanilla or lemon extract
> 48 blueberries (about 1 pint)

Preheat the oven to 350 degrees.

Sugarcoat and butter an 8-hole muffin tin; set aside.

Beat the eggs and sugar. Sift in the flour and baking powder and blend. Add the butter and vanilla extract and mix.

Spoon the batter into the muffin tins up to ¼" from the top of each mold. Place 6 blueberries on top of each muffin. Bake for 15–20 minutes. Unmold and serve hot with a little pat of butter in the middle.

SERVES 4.

FRENCH TOAST WITH A TWIST

2 eggs
¾ cup milk
1 teaspoon cinnamon
zest of ½ orange
¼ teaspoon allspice
1 teaspoon dark rum
½ teaspoon vanilla extract
¼ cup sugar
2 tablespoons peanut oil
4 slices white bread

Beat the eggs in a bowl large enough to fit the bread slices. Mix in the milk and ½ teaspoon of the cinnamon. Add the orange zest, allspice, rum, and vanilla extract.

Blend together the sugar and the remaining cinnamon in a cup; set aside.

Heat the oil in a large skillet.

Dip each bread slice into the egg mixture and coat each side, allowing the bread to soak up the mixture. Cook in the hot skillet on each side until golden brown.

Use a wide spatula to remove the French toast from the skillet; drain on paper towels. Place on a serving dish and sprinkle with the sugar-cinnamon mixture, or, if you prefer, top with warm maple syrup. Serve immediately.

SERVES 2.

GOLDEN SLICES

1 egg white
5 tablespoons confectioners' sugar
1 teaspoon fresh lemon juice
1 country pound cake (page 60)

Preheat the oven to 350 degrees.

Combine the egg white and the sugar in a large mixing bowl. Blend in the lemon juice.

Cut the cake into ½ inch thick slices and spread them on a cookie sheet. Brush the top of each slice with the egg white mixture. Bake for 10 minutes until golden brown. Remove from the cookie sheet and serve. These also make delicious tea or coffee snacks.

SERVES 8.

PETITE TARTE SÈCHE

1½ cups flour
3 tablespoons sugar
3 tablespoons unsalted butter, room temperature
3 tablespoons virgin olive oil
¼ teaspoon salt
2 eggs
2 quarts boiling water
¼ cup brown sugar

Preheat the oven to 350 degrees.

Sift the flour and the sugar together in a medium size mixing bowl. Add the butter, the oil, and the salt. Combine with a wooden spoon, or with your hands. Beat the eggs in a separate bowl; add them slowly to the flour mixture, using your hands to mold the ingredients into a soft mound. Sprinkle the dough with flour. Refrigerate for 1 hour.

Flour your work surface. This is a very moist, elastic dough, easier to work by hand than with a rolling pin. Flatten it to a ¼" thickness. Use a pizza wheel cutter to slice it into 1" × 4" strips. Freeze any leftover dough for use later. Carefully lift the pastry strips with a spatula onto a platter lined with wax paper.

In a large saucepan, bring to a boil 2 quarts of water. With a spatula, gently lower the pastry strips into the boiling water. With a large slotted spoon, remove them as soon as they rise to the surface; drain on a platter lined with paper towels.

Butter a large cookie sheet and lay the pastry strips on it. Sprinkle each strip with some of the brown sugar. Bake until golden brown, about 10–12 minutes.

SERVES 6.

SOPHISTICATED BROWNIES

3 cups shelled pecans
4 slices white bread
2 heaped tablespoons cocoa powder
4 tablespoons chocolate syrup
6 tablespoons sugar
4 egg yolks
4 egg whites
2 tablespoons melted, unsalted butter
2 tablespoons Amaretto liqueur

Preheat the oven to 300 degrees.

Butter and sugarcoat a 1½ quart baking dish; set aside.

In the bowl of a processor, process 2 cups of the pecans and the bread slices into fine crumbs. Pour into a mixing bowl. Add the cocoa powder, the chocolate syrup, 4 tablespoons of the sugar, and the egg yolks and mix with a rubber spatula. Stir in the remaining nuts, the butter, and the Amaretto; set aside.

Beat the egg whites with an electric mixer until soft peaks form. Add 2 tablespoons of sugar and beat until the peaks become stiff.

Fold the egg whites into the chocolate mixture. Pour the mixture into the baking dish. Bake for 20 minutes. Unmold and allow to cool before serving. These brownies give an exciting twist to a traditional American treat.

SERVES 8.

STRAWBERRY NAPOLITAIN

demi-feuilletage pastry (page 15)
1 egg
2 tablespoons water
½ cup fresh or frozen strawberries
1 cup crème pâtissière (page 19)
1 teaspoon confectioners' sugar

Preheat the oven to 350 degrees.

Butter a large cookie sheet; set aside.

Roll out a 10" × 15", ½" thick square of pastry dough on a floured work space. Cut the dough into five 3" strips. Place them on the cookie sheet; set aside.

Mix the egg and 2 tablespoons of water together in a cup. Brush the top of the pastry strips with the egg wash. Bake for 25 minutes.

Remove the pastry strips from the oven and slice them in half horizontally with a sharp, serrated knife. Return them to the oven and bake again for 10 minutes until the crust is browned and completely dry inside. Set aside to cool.

In a mixing bowl with a rubber spatula mash the berries into the cream. Spoon a small amount of the berry-cream mixture onto a pastry strip. Cover with a second pastry strip; top with a small amount of the cream. Repeat this step for the remaining crème pâtissière and pastry strips, finishing with a pastry strip on top. Sprinkle with confectioners' sugar and refrigerate until ready to serve. Use a sharp, serrated knife to slice the napolitain into 4 equal pieces.

SERVES 4.

CHAPTER 9
COOKIES

LANGUES DE CHAT

½ cup unsalted butter, room temperature
1 cup sugar
6 egg whites, about ⅔ cup
1 cup flour
1 teaspoon vanilla extract

Preheat the oven to 350 degrees.
    Place the butter and sugar into the bowl of a food processor. Process until smooth and creamy. Add the egg whites and process again for 20 seconds; pour into a large bowl. Mix in the flour with a spatula, then the vanilla extract.
    Use the spatula to spoon the mixture into a pastry bag with a size 10 tube opening. Use a non-stick cookie sheet, or one covered with wax paper. Squeeze out rows of 2"-long cookies leaving 1" spaces between each cookie.
    Bake just until the edges, not the entire cookie, turn brown; about 8 minutes. Remove from the oven and allow to cool on the cookie sheet before serving. These light cookies go well with tea, coffee, and ice cream.

MAKES ABOUT 40 COOKIES.

FLORENTINES

1 cup sugar
3 tablespoons unsalted butter, room temperature
½ cup heavy cream
3 tablespoons honey
1 cup finely ground hazelnuts
1 cup finely ground, blanched almonds
1 tablespoon almonds finely ground into powder

Preheat the oven to 200 degrees.

Place the sugar, butter, heavy cream, and honey into a large saucepan and bring to a boil over a medium flame. Reduce the heat and continue to simmer until the mixture thickens to a syrup-like consistency and turns brown.

Remove the liquid mixture from the heat. Mix in the nut crumbs and the almond powder. Set aside to cool slightly.

Roll out a 16"-long sheet of wax paper on a flat surface. Pour the mixture onto the paper. Cover with another 16"-long sheet. Use a rolling pin to flatten to a ⅛" thickness. Refrigerate about 2 minutes to cool and stiffen the florentine sheet.

Remove from the refrigerator and score 1"-wide squares with a pizza cutter. Be sure to do this before the florentine cools too much and becomes too hard. Break the scored cookie squares and arrange them on a Teflon-coated cookie sheet, 2 inches apart. Bake for 5 minutes. The cookies should melt, spread, and become an even golden color. Allow to cool on the cookie sheet before serving.

MAKES ABOUT 15 COOKIES.

PETER'S BUTTERFLIES (PAPILLONS)

½ cup sugar
1 puff pastry or demi-feuilletage pastry (page 15)

Preheat the oven to 375 degrees.

Cover your work surface with sugar. Roll out the pastry dough to a ¼"-thick 12" × 10" rectangle; sprinkle with additional sugar. Use the rolling pin to press the sugar into the pastry.

Fold the sides of the pastry inward lengthwise so that the edges touch in the center. Roll out to a ¼" thickness. Repeat the last 2 steps, then place on a cookie sheet and refrigerate for 20 minutes. This hardens the dough and makes it easier to cut.

Remove the dough from the refrigerator and return it to your work surface. Use a sharp knife to slice the sheet of dough into ½" × 3" pieces.

Cover the cookie sheet with a sheet of wax paper. Place the slices of dough on the cookie sheet 1" apart. Refrigerate for another 10–15 minutes, then bake for 10–12 minutes. Allow to cool before serving with tea, coffee, or ice cream.

MAKES ABOUT 40 COOKIES.

PETER'S MADELEINES

½ cup almond powder processed from whole almonds
¼ cup flour
¾ cup confectioners' sugar
1½ teaspoons honey
4 egg whites
½ cup unsalted butter, melted

Preheat the oven to 350 degrees.

Place the dry ingredients into the bowl of a food processor. Add the honey and the egg whites; process until smooth. Add the melted butter and process again about 10 seconds.

Butter your favorite 2″ cookie molds. Spoon the mixture into each of the molds. Bake for 20–25 minutes. Allow the cookies to cool, then serve alone as a main dessert, or as a snack with buttermilk, tea, or coffee.

MAKES ABOUT 25–30 2″ COOKIES.

JEAN-MICHEL'S COCONUT COOKIES

>⅔ cup shredded coconut
>1 cup sugar
>5 egg whites
>1 egg
>1 teaspoon arrowroot

Preheat the oven to 350 degrees.

In a large bowl, mix together the coconut and the sugar. Stir in the egg whites. Add the egg and the arrowroot.

Using a tablespoon, spread spoon-size balls of the mixture on a non-stick cookie sheet (leave 2" between each). Use your hand to flatten them into oval shapes. Bake for 15 minutes. Cool on the cookie sheet before serving.

MAKES ABOUT 30 COOKIES.

LEMON COOKIES

½ cup soft, unsalted butter
½ cup sugar
2 eggs
½ cup flour
juice of 1 lemon

Preheat the oven to 300 degrees.

In a large bowl, whisk the butter and the sugar until it becomes creamy. Add the eggs. Sift in the flour and beat. Add the lemon juice.

Spoon the batter into a pastry bag with a medium size tube. Squeeze out the cookies (about 2 teaspoons' worth) onto a lightly buttered cookie sheet leaving 1" between each. Bake for 14 minutes until the cookies are lightly browned. Cool on the cookie sheet before serving.

MAKES ABOUT 60 SMALL COOKIES.

CRISPY VANILLA COOKIES

2 cups flour
6 egg yolks
1 entire egg
½ cup soft butter, cut into small morsels
1 cup sugar
1 teaspoon vanilla extract
½ teaspoon baking powder

GLAZE:
1 egg yolk
1 tablespoon water

Preheat the oven to 350 degrees.

Sift the flour into a large mixing bowl. Using your hands, mix in the egg yolks, the egg, the butter, the sugar, the vanilla extract, and the baking powder. Use your hands to mix the ingredients. Form the dough into a ball. Refrigerate for 1 hour.

Butter a large cookie sheet. Flour your work surface. Remove the dough from the refrigerator and roll it out to ¼" thickness. Use your favorite 2" cookie cutter to cut out the cookies. Place them 1" apart on the cookie sheet. Rake a sharp knife across the top of the dough to create designs.

Glaze: Mix the egg yolk and the water in a small bowl. Brush the glaze over the top of the cookies. Bake for 50 minutes. Roll any leftover dough into a ball and return it to the refrigerator. It can be stored up to 2 to 3 days.

MAKES ABOUT 40 MEDIUM SIZE COOKIES.

CHAPTER 10
CONSERVES AND DRINKS

PUNCH AU CAFÉ

In cold weather, this spiced-up coffee can be served hot as an after-dinner punch. In the summertime, add ice to it to make a refreshing iced coffee.

> 2 eggs
> ½ cup sugar
> ¼ teaspoon nutmeg
> ¼ teaspoon allspice
> ¼ teaspoon cinnamon
> 2 tablespoons rum
> 2 cups milk
> 1 vanilla bean, split
> 1 cup coffee

Whisk the eggs and the sugar in a large mixing bowl. Add the nutmeg, allspice, cinnamon, and rum; blend and set aside.

Heat the milk and the vanilla bean in a saucepan over a medium flame. Add the coffee and bring the mixture to a boil.

Stir the boiling milk into the sugar–rum mixture. Serve immediately in 4-oz. mugs.

SERVES 6.

YOGURT MINT JULEP

1 tablespoon fresh mint, chopped
32 ounces plain yogurt
10 ounces ginger ale
1 tablespoon sugar

Whisk the mint and the yogurt in a large mixing bowl. Add the ginger ale and the sugar and mix. Refrigerate until ready to use. Serve chilled in 6-oz. mugs.

MAKES 6–7 CUPS.

RASPBERRY WINE

1 bottle dry white wine
3 tablespoons port
3 tablespoons raspberry brandy
1 tablespoon sugar
1 pint fresh raspberries

Over a medium flame, bring to a boil for 1 minute the wine, the port, the brandy, and the sugar in a large saucepan.

Spoon the fruit into a bottle large enough to hold 3–4 cups of liquid. Using a funnel, pour the hot wine mixture over the fruit, filling the bottle up to its neck. Close the bottle tightly, then set aside for 4–5 hours before refrigerating. Serve cold with desserts, or as an apéritif.

SERVES 8.

MILK SHAKE

1 quart lowfat buttermilk
2 tablespoons sugar
1 teaspoon vanilla extract
⅛ teaspoon cinnamon
⅛ teaspoon nutmeg
2 cloves, crushed
1 egg (optional)

Place all of the ingredients into a large mixing bowl. Whisk them together just until bubbles appear. Refrigerate until ready for use. Serve chilled or over ice cubes in 6-oz. glasses.

MAKES 5–6 GLASSES.

HOT OR COLD WINE SOUP

½ cup dry white wine
¾ cup sugar
1 vanilla bean, split
3 cloves
5 cups hot water
½ pound dried apple slices, cut in thin strips
½ pound dried peach slices, cut in thin strips
2 slices dried pineapple, cut in thin strips
½ pound dried apricots, sliced in half
½ cup golden raisins
½ cup dark raisins

Place the wine, sugar, vanilla bean, and cloves into a large saucepan. Pour in 5 cups of hot water and bring the mixture to a boil.

Meanwhile, cut the apple, peaches, and pineapple slices in thin strips and put into a large bowl. Add this to the ingredients already boiling in the saucepan. Continue to cook over a high flame for 5–6 minutes more.

Add the halved apricots and all the raisins to the saucepan; cook 5 minutes more.

Pour this mixture into a large soup bowl. During hot summer months, serve this fruit soup cold with whipped cream (page 17). In cold weather, serve still hot.

CHAPTER 11
DESSERTS FOR CHILDREN

MY FIRST CHOCOLATE CAKE

This is the cake that I made for my sister's birthday when I was five years old. It needs no cooking, and is extremely simple to prepare. It was my very first cake, and is still one of my favorites.

>5 slices white bread
>8 tablespoons chocolate syrup
>2 tablespoons natural yogurt
>3 tablespoons hazelnut spread
>2 tablespoons soft, unsalted butter

Remove the crust and break the bread slices into small pieces in a bowl. Stir in the chocolate syrup, the yogurt, the hazelnut spread, and the butter. Refrigerate for 45 minutes before serving.

SERVES 4.

COCONUT VELVET

Recipes for children should be simple, fun to make, and, of course, good-tasting. This cool, refreshing dessert, served straight from the refrigerator, requires no cooking, and makes a wonderful party treat or after dinner dish.

> 1 cup natural, plain yogurt
> 2 cups shredded coconut
> 2 egg yolks
> ¼ cup sugar
> ¼ cup melted, unsalted butter, room temperature

Needed: Six 3½″ × 1½″ bowls or ramekins.

Beat the yogurt, the coconut, the egg yolks, and the sugar in a bowl. Stir in the butter. Spoon into the ramekins. Refrigerate for 3 hours. Serve alone or with cookies.

SERVES 6.

A LITTLE MOUSE

This cute dessert is so easy that, with just a little help from you, children as young as three years old can make it.

>2 canned pear halves in light syrup
>4 whole cloves
>2 ¼" wide × 2" long orange peels
>4 roasted, blanched almond slices

Place each pear half, flat side down, on a dessert plate. Insert 2 cloves 1" apart, ½" from the narrow ends of the pear halves (the top when the pear is standing upright) to form the mouse's eyes. Vertically insert 1 almond ½" behind each clove to form the ears. Place the orange peels beneath the large end of each pear to form the tails. Serve alone or with a raspberry sauce (page 21) or crème anglaise (page 18).

SERVES 2.

PEANUT BUTTER MUFFINS

½ cup creamy, unsalted peanut butter
2 tablespoons sugar
¼ cup lightly toasted wheat germ
2 whole eggs
¼ teaspoon baking powder
2 egg whites

Preheat the oven to 350 degrees.
Needed: Two miniature muffin pans, each with 12 1½" cups.
Butter the muffin pans; set aside.
Beat the peanut butter, 1 tablespoon of the sugar, the wheat germ, and the eggs in a medium size bowl. Add the baking powder; set aside.
Beat the egg whites with an electric mixer until soft peaks form. Add 1 tablespoon of sugar and beat until the peaks become stiff. Fold into the peanut butter mixture.
Spoon the mixture just to the top of each muffin cup. Bake 12 minutes. Unmold and serve warm.

MAKES 24 SMALL MUFFINS.

INDEX

almonds:
   Almond Milk Pudding, 54
   Very Light Almond Cake, 53
apples:
   Apple Beignets, 84
   Apple Sauce, 22
   Caramelized Apple Tart, 65
   Cinnamon Apple Pudding, 75
   Country Tart, 66
   filling for tart shells, 72
   Fruit Clafoutis, 83
   Tarte Tatin, 69
   Whole Wheat Apple Cake, 49
apricots:
   Potato and Apricot Gratin, 86
   Potato and Apricot Pannequet, 77
   Rice Crown with Fresh Apricots, 46
   sauce, 23

bain-marie, 11
baking dishes, 13
bananas, Ruth's pudding, 87
beignets, 25
   apple, 84
belt, ladyfinger, 26

berries:
   Blueberry Muffins, 99
   filling for tart circles, 73
   Frozen Fruit Soufflé, 95
   Fruit Clafoutis, 83
   Raspberry Sauce, 21
   Raspberry Wine, 115
   Strawberry Napolitain, 104
   Strawberry Sauce, 21
beverages:
   Milk Shake, 116
   Punch au Café, 113
   Raspberry Wine, 115
   Yogurt Mint Julep, 114
blanch, 11
Blueberry Muffins, 99
book stands, 13
Bread Pudding à l'Orange, 59
breads:
   Blueberry Muffins, 99
   French Toast with a Twist, 100
   Lemon Bread, 31
   Peanut Butter Muffins, 122
   Petite Tarte Sèche, 102
   Raisin and Rum Bread, 43
   Spice Bread, 63
Breakfast treats, 99–104
Brioche Trompe l'Oeil, 32
brownies, sophisticated, 103
butter and sugarcoat, 11

cake pans, 13
cakes:
  Brioche Trompe l'Oeil, 32
  Chocolate Chip Cake, 35
  Chocolate Potato Cake, 79
  Coconut Cake, 29
  Country Pound Cake, 60
  Country Prune Flan, 40
  Crunchy Hazelnut Cake, 44
  Eric's Chocolate Cake, 51
  Light Cheesecake, 38
  My First Chocolate Cake, 119
  My Grandmother's Chocolate Cake, 62
  Orange Chocolate Chip Cake, 37
  Pineapple Cake, 47
  Plaisir des Abeilles, 30
  Roulé à la Vanille, 45
  Very Light Almond Cake, 53
  Very Simple Génoise Cake, 20
  Walnut Cake, 50
  White Cornmeal Cake, 48
  White Wine Cake, 34
  Whole Wheat Apple Cake, 49
  Yogurt Cake, 57
Caramel, 42
  Caramel Pudding, 44
  Caramel Sauce, 21
  Caramelized Apple Tart, 65
Carrot Tourte, 52
casseroles, 14
cheesecake, light, 38
Chestnut Mousseline, 42
children, desserts for:
  Coconut Velvet, 120
  Little Mouse, 121
  My First Chocolate Cake, 119
  Peanut Butter Muffins, 122
chocolate:
  Chocolate Chip Cake, 35
  Chocolate and Pine Kernel Tart, 68
  Chocolate Potato Cake, 79
  Eric's Chocolate Cake, 51
  My First Chocolate Cake, 119
  My Grandmother's Chocolate Cake, 62
  Orange Chocolate Chip Cake, 37
  Sophisticated Brownies, 103
Cinnamon Apple Pudding, 75
clafoutis, fruit, 83
cobbler, Mollie's peach, 85
Coconut Cake, 29
Coconut Cookies, 109
Coconut Velvet, 120
coffee, Punch au Café, 113
cookie sheets, 14
cookies:
  Crispy Vanilla Cookies, 111
  Florentines, 106
  Jean-Michel's Coconut Cookies, 109
  Langues de Chat, 105
  Lemon Cookies, 110
  Peter's Butterflies, 107
  Peter's Madeleines, 108
Country Pound Cake, 60
Country Prune Flan, 40
Country Tart, 66
Crème Anglaise, 18
Crème Brûlée, 36
Crème Pâtissière, 19
Crêpes, 89
  Crêpe à l'Orange, 91

Crêpe Soufflé, 91
　made with water, 90
Crépinette, pineapple, 97
Crispy Vanilla Cookies, 111
Crunchy Hazelnut Cake, 44
custards:
　Crème Brûlée, 36
　See also Puddings

Demi-feuilletage Pastry
　Dough, 15
Diplomate Minute, 41
Diplomate au Poire, 58
dorure, 11
La Douceur de Tante Adele, 61
dried fruits, Hot or Cold Wine
　Soup, 117

Easy Pâte à Beignet, 25
egg wash, 11
electric mixers, 14
Eric's Chocolate Cake, 51

fillings:
　Crème Pâtissière, 19
　for Tea Tart Shells, 72–73
flan, country prune, 40
Florentines, 106
food processors, 14
freezing of pastry dough, 16
French Toast with a Twist, 100
fritters, plantain, 78
Frozen Fruit Soufflé, 95
fruits:
　Apple Beignets, 84
　Apple Sauce, 22
　Blueberry Muffins, 99
　Bread Pudding à l'Orange, 59

Caramelized Apple Tart, 65
Cinnamon Apple Pudding, 75
Country Prune Flan, 40
Country Tart, 66
Crêpe à l'Orange, 91
Diplomate au Poire, 58
filling for tart circles, 73
fillings for Tea Tart Shells, 72
Frozen Fruit Soufflé, 95
Fruit Clafoutis, 83
Fruit Soufflés, 94
Hot or Cold Wine Soup, 117
Lemon Tart, 70
Little Mouse, 121
Mollie's Peach Cobbler, 85
Orange Bavaroise, 88
Orange Chocolate Chip
　Cake, 37
Orange Sweets, 55
Orange Tart, 4
Plum Sauce, 23
Poached Pear, 24
Potato and Apricot Gratin, 86
Potato and Apricot Panne-
　quet, 77
Raspberry Wine, 115
Rice Crown with Fresh
　Apricots, 46
Ruth's Banana Pudding, 87
Strawberry Napolitain, 104
Strawberry Sauce, 21
Tarte Tatin, 69
Whole Wheat Apple Cake, 49

garnishes for tart circles, 73
génoise cake, 20

glacé, 11
Golden Slices, 101
Grandmother's Chocolate Cake, 62
gratins:
   Potato and Apricot Gratin, 86
   Sweet Potato Gratin, 81

hazelnut cake, 44
Hot or Cold Wine Soup, 117
hot-water bath, 11
hygiene, 12–13

ice cream, vanilla, 39
individual soufflés, 93
ingredients, 13

Jean-Michel's Coconut Cookies, 109

Ladyfingers, 26
Langues de Chat, 105
leftovers, Bread Pudding à l'Orange, 59
Lemon Bread, 31
Lemon Cookies, 110
Lemon Soufflé, 94
Lemon Tart, 70
Light Cheesecake, 38
Little Mouse, 121

madeleines, Peter's, 108
Milk Shake, 116
mint julep, yogurt, 114
mixers, 14
mixing bowls, 14
molds, 14
   Cinnamon Apple Pudding, 75
   La Douceur de Tante Adele, 61

Rice Crown with Fresh Apricots, 46
Mollie's Peach Cobbler, 85
mousseline, chestnut, 42
muffins:
   Blueberry Muffins, 99
   Peanut Butter Muffins, 122
My First Chocolate Cake, 119
My Grandmother's Chocolate Cake, 62

nectarines:
   sauce, 23
   tart filling, 72

odors, to remove, 13
Omelette Soufflé, 96
oranges:
   Crêpe à l'Orange, 91
   Orange Bavaroise, 88
   Orange Chocolate Chip Cake, 37
   Orange Sweets, 55
   Orange Tart, 4
   tart filling, 72

papillons, Peter's Butterflies, 107
Parmentier, Antoine Augustin, 80
pastry, to prepare, 12–13
pastry dough:
   Demi-feuilletage, 15
   Pâte Brisée, 16–17
Pâte à Beignet, 25
Pâte Brisée, 16–17
peaches:
   Fruit Clafoutis, 83
   Mollie's Peach Cobbler, 85
Peanut Butter Muffins, 122
pears:
   Diplomate au Poire, 58

filling for tart circles, 73
Fruit Clafoutis, 83
Little Mouse, 121
Poached Pear, 24
Petals des Roses Soufflé, 94
Peter's Butterflies, 107
Peter's Madeleines, 108
Petite Tarte Sèche, 102
Petites Florentines Parmentier, 80
Pine Kernel and Chocolate Tart, 68
Pineapple Cake, 47
Pineapple Crépinette, 97
Pistachio Puddings, 33
Plaisir des Abeilles, 30
Plantain Fritters, 78
plums:
    Fruit Clafoutis, 83
    Plum Sauce, 23
Poached Pear, 24
Potato and Apricot Gratin, 86
Potato and Apricot Pannequet, 77
Petites Florentines Parmentier, 80
pound cake, 60
    Golden Slices, 101
precooked pastry shells, 16
pricking with a fork, 11
prunes:
    Country Prune Flan, 40
    filling for tart circles, 73
puddings:
    Almond Milk Pudding, 54
    Bread Pudding à l'Orange, 59
    Caramel Pudding, 44
    Cinnamon Apple Pudding, 75
    Diplomate Minute, 41
    Diplomate au Poire, 58

Pistachio Puddings, 33
Rice Crown with Fresh Apricots, 46
Ruth's Banana Pudding, 87
See also Custards
Punch au Café, 113

Raisin and Rum Bread, 43
Raspberry Soufflé, 94
Raspberry Wine, 115
Rhubarb Tart, 67
Rice Crown with Fresh Apricots, 46
rolling pins, 14
rose-petal soufflé, 94
Roulé à la Vanille, 45
rum and raisin bread, 43
Ruth's Banana Pudding, 87

saucepans, 14
sauces:
    Apple Sauce, 22
    Caramel Sauce, 21
    Crème Anglaise, 18
    Crème Pâtissière, 19
    Lemon Butter, 31
    Plum Sauce, 23
    Raspberry Sauce, 21
    Strawberry Sauce, 21
    Whipped Cream, 17
        topping for cheesecake, 38
sauté pans, 14
shells:
    Tea Tart Shells, 71
    tulip-shaped, 27
skim, 11
Sophisticated Brownies, 103
soufflé molds, 14
soufflés, 92
    Frozen Fruit Soufflé, 95
    Fruit Soufflés, 94
    Omelette Soufflé, 96

Soufflé with Fresh Thyme, 93
soup, wine and fruit, 117
sour cream, whipped, 17
Spice Bread, 63
springform pans, 13
strainers, 14
Strawberry Napolitain, 104
Strawberry Sauce, 21
Sweet Potato Gratin, 81

tart pans, 13
Tarte Tatin, 69
  sour cream topping, 17
tarts:
  Caramelized Apple Tart, 65
  Carrot Tourte, 52
  Chocolate and Pine Kernel Tart, 68
  Country Tart, 66
  Lemon Tart, 70
  Orange Tart, 74
  Rhubarb Tart, 67
  shells, 71–73
  Tarte Tatin, 69
  Tomato Tourte, 82
Tea Tart Shells, 71
temperatures, 12
thyme, soufflé with, 93
timing note, 12
Tomato Tourte, 82
toppings. *See* Sauces
Tulip Shells, 27

unmold mold, 11
utensils, 13–14

vanilla cookies, crispy, 111
Vanilla Ice Cream, 39
vanilla roulé, 45
vegetables:
  Carrot Tourte, 52
  Chocolate Potato Cake, 79
  Petites Florentines Parmentier, 80
  Plantain Fritters, 78
  Potato and Apricot Gratin, 86
  Potato and Apricot Pannequet, 77
  Sweet Potato Gratin, 81
  Tomato Tourte, 82
Very Light Almond Cake, 53
Very Simple Génoise Cake, 20
vocabulary, 11–12

Walnut Cake, 50
Whipped Cream, 17
  topping for cheesecake, 38
White Cornmeal Cake, 48
White Wine Cake, 34
Whole Wheat Apple Cake, 49
wine, raspberry, 115
wine soup, hot or cold, 117
work space, 12

Yogurt Cake, 57
Yogurt Mint Julep, 114

zest, 12